Teaching Young Children Mathematics

Teaching Young Children
Mathematics

Sydney L. Schwartz

TEACHING YOUNG CHILDREN

Doris Pronin Fromberg and Leslie R. Williams

Series Editors

Westport, Connecticut
London

Library of Congress Cataloging-in-Publication Data

Schwartz, Sydney L. (Sydney Lisbeth)
    Teaching young children mathematics / Sydney L. Schwartz.
      p. cm.—(Teaching young children, ISSN 1554-6004)
    Includes bibliographical references and index.
    ISBN 0–275–98216–5 (alk. paper)
    1. Mathematics—Study and teaching (Primary)—United States. 2.
Mathematics—Study and teaching (Elementary)—United States. 3.
Mathematics—Study and teaching—Parent participation—United States.
I. Title. II. Series.
QA135.6.S437 2005
372.7—dc22   2005013515

British Library Cataloguing in Publication Data is available.

Library of Congress Catalog Card Number: 2005013515
ISBN: 0–275–98216–5
ISSN: 1554–6004

First published in 2005

Praeger Publishers, 88 Post Road West, Westport, CT 06881
An imprint of Greenwood Publishing Group, Inc.
www.praeger.com

Printed in the United States of America

The paper used in this book complies with the
Permanent Paper Standard issued by the National
Information Standards Organization (Z39.48–1984).

10 9 8 7 6 5 4 3 2 1

Contents

Preface

The Challenge of Early Childhood Mathematics Education

The text of this book grows out of this author's unending effort to increasingly understand the complex elements that bind teaching and learning, in this case related to mathematics. As a novice teacher, first with four-year-olds, followed by three-, five-, six-year-olds and on up, I discovered there is no one route to connecting with learners. While they offer a number of windows through which we may view their learning base—that is, their knowledge, understandings, skills, and beliefs—translating that information into plans for teaching and learning is very complicated. The other part of this professional challenge, I discovered, was my own limited understanding of the curriculum content. Although, by conventional standards, I was an excellent mathematics student all through my school years, I never really engaged in *mathematical* thinking until I participated in an advanced graduate course in elementary school mathematics. Only then did light bulbs flash, and I became excited about this new world I was discovering. When I began working with teachers, I realized they, too, were struggling with the same set of challenges.

My search led me to think about what children are learning when they get involved in an activity of their own choosing. What mathematics patterns are they discovering, and what skills are they using? Equally important was the answer to the question, "How do I know?" I began to understand that there are many faces to an emerging discovery of mathematical relationships and patterns within an event, and I found myself dwelling on the common knowledge that is bedded in different activities.

In this book, I have focused on bringing to life ideas about mathematics teaching and learning by sharing with readers many classroom experiences that serve to make connections between important learning goals and the interactions in an educational environment. During the writing process, I have revisited my own professional journey, beginning with initial work with three-, four-, and five-year-old children and culminating with teachers of preprimary and primary children. Over the years, ideas were born, tested out in the real world of children, revised, and extended. The journey goes on.

This book addresses needs for both preprimary and primary teachers to empower young children to understand and use mathematics. For the preprimary teacher, it addresses the need to support young children's emerging mathematics understanding and skills in action-based prekindergarten and kindergarten classrooms in a context which conforms with current knowledge about the way young children learn mathematics. For the primary teacher in grades 1 and 2, it addresses the need to connect the formalized mathematics curriculum to the daily lives of children so that they will use and value their growing mathematics understandings and skills.

Several themes influence what I have written. I view mathematics education as an area shaped by three major interwoven fields of knowledge:

1. mathematics content—the hierarchy of big ideas and how they are connected;

2. the processes by which children learn mathematics during the early childhood years; and

3. the instructional options for fostering mathematics learning, including both the teaching role and curriculum activities.

The key phrases that speak to my commitments are "supporting mathematics content learning" and "through children's interests." My early struggles with curriculum for preprimary children flowed from a limited knowledge of the big ideas in mathematics. I was committed to providing an action-based, interest-centered program but lacked sufficient knowledge of the content to serve as an instructional agent to bridge their high-interest activity and the mathematics possibilities. Organized presentation of subject matter content took a back seat to my search for ways to connect with the children's expressed interests. The idea of conducting "lessons" presented serious challenges to my ideas about following children's lead.

Almost in desperation, I spent a great deal of time observing children in action and listening to their conversations so I could present material and experiences that added to their interests. Over time I learned how to build experiences with mathematical content on what children already knew. I discovered the content—process connections and found ways to engage and sustain children's involvement in active learning experiences in which mathematics was an integral part.

Throughout this book I share much of what I have learned in almost five decades not only of teaching but also of learning from children. This book is about addressing the need for more effective mathematics education for young children through connecting content and process, teaching and learning, and capitalizing on the many ways that mathematics serves and enriches our lives.

Addressing the Need for Early Mathematics Education: A Preview

Chapter 1, "The Educational Challenge," discusses some of the critical elements of the educational challenge of early mathematics education and a little bit of the historical context.

Chapter 2, "Designing Games and Playful Activities," addresses one of the most pressing public demands of schooling—that is, to increase speed and accuracy in using mathematics in and out of the classroom. In this chapter, the development of accuracy and fluency in computation, shape and space geometry, and measurement is coordinated with our cultural enthusiasm for playing games.

Chapters 3, 4, and 5 delve into the connections between what we know about how children learn and the foundational content—the big ideas—that constitute the early stages of learning about number, geometry and measurement. These chapters identify important concepts that govern what we know about the sequence of learning and mathematical content.

Chapter 3, "How Young Children Learn Mathematics," discusses the major views held about early childhood mathematical development and learning. Each view implies distinctive guidelines on which teachers make decisions about instruction. This chapter identifies and discusses the implications of each view that serves as a foundation to guide adults in developing experiences empowering young children to become mathematical thinkers and doers.

Chapter 4, "How Young Children Learn Number Concepts and Skills," looks at young children's developing mathematical number sense. Young children take a predictable journey from initial awareness of numerical quantity to understanding and performing computations with confidence. This chapter defines the major map points along the route. There are descriptions of the many ways that children engage in using mathematics at each stage of the journey. A content map defines the progression of development in number skills and understandings that further the process–content connections.

Chapter 5, "How Young Children Learn Geometry and Measurement," continues to consider how young children develop mathematical knowledge and skills, with a focus now on geometry and measurement. Shape and space are dimensions of children's worlds. Their understanding of the patterns and relationships in form, position, and location are continually refined by using informal and formal measurement strategies. As with number, there is a predictable sequence in the development of understanding and the acquisition of skills in these two areas of mathematics.

Chapters 6 and 7 deal with some of the complex dimensions of "teaching." They examine major considerations for making instructional decisions.

In Chapter 6, "The Connection between Assessment and Teaching," instructional strategies are coordinated with each of three purposes: (1) introducing new learning, (2) practicing skills and testing knowledge, and (3) applying and extending knowledge and skills. Assessment information is the basis for adults to plan different formats for teaching. The generic purposes include (1) adult support for the acquisition of new content and processes, (2) opportunities to practice skills and test understanding in order to improve speed and accuracy, and (3) application of skills and understandings in valued activities.

Chapter 7, "How Adults Can Communicate with Young Children about Mathematics," explores the nature of authentic communication and the variety of messages adults send to children through "teacher talk" that support and/or limit efforts by children to achieve autonomy in successfully using mathematics in their lives.

Chapters 8, 9, and 10 connect content and process with curriculum, beginning with time-management tools followed by a focus on integrating mathematics with science and then with social studies.

Chapter 8, "Calendars and Clocks," describes and illustrates an approach to constructing calendars and clocks with children in ways that make sense to them and in the process making calendars and clocks useful tools in their daily lives.

Chapter 9, "Science and Mathematics," describes activities for collecting and recording data that constitute a major link between science and mathematics. This chapter discusses approaches to data collection by young children.

Chapter 10, "Social Studies and Mathematics," continues the process of examining how number and data collection, geometry, and measurement are integrated into social studies activities.

The final two chapters take the long view about learning mathematics in meaningful contexts.

Chapter 11, "Meaningful Use of Mathematics in Classroom Routines," explores a variety of ways that mathematics can serve as a tool to develop a cooperative social environment in which children and adults collaborate in meeting the everyday classroom management needs. It features the many strategies adults have developed to use mathematics in order to enhance children's autonomy and social responsibility in groups.

Chapter 12, "Putting It All Together," brings together the variety of perspectives that can create a high-quality mathematics education for young children from birth to eight years of age. The illustration features a geography unit.

It is important to note that my focus on tuning in to children as active learners also embraces special needs of children for whom there is a greater distance between the mainstream group and their life's experiences. While it is true that those who work with English-language learners, youngsters growing up in cultures other than that of the class group, and children with physical and social handicaps need information and instructional skills to meet the additional challenges presented by these groups, the developmental sequences and instructional design ideas are integral to teaching mathematics to all children. The challenge to link mathematics learning to children's interests defines the challenge of early childhood mathematics education.

Many persons have contributed to this work, to whom I wish to express my deep appreciation. First, to my series editor, Doris Fromberg, who not only invited me to share my views about teaching young children mathematics, but also offered the kind of encouragement and help so often needed in the writing process. Secondly, to my valued colleague Frances Curcio, who brought me into the mathematics community in so many different ways. Through her continuing invitations to join in different mathematical initiatives here and abroad, I was able to bring the voice of early childhood to the mathematics community and bring the voice of mathematics to the early childhood community. Collaborations with David Whitin, a former colleague now at Wayne State University, enriched my understanding of the possibilities for mathematics education with teachers of young children. Finally, I am deeply grateful for the ongoing support of Anna Beth Brown and Sherry Copeland, who read and reread the drafts and made valuable suggestions to improve clarity. I am not able to directly thank the many children, teachers, and colleagues who have contributed to the development of my ideas, but I feel very fortunate to have had such a rich set of experiences in my professional career.

CHAPTER 1

The Educational Challenge

Empowering Young Children to
Use Mathematics

The primary goal of mathematics education is to support the development of fluency in mathematics in a variety of life's situations. Children show us, in so many ways, that mathematics learning begins long before mathematics *education* begins.

Emerging Mathematicians

A two-year-old chants to herself in the bathtub, "splish, splish, oh-oh, splish, splish, oh-oh" while simultaneously squeezing the water out of a rubber toy. With each "splish" she squeezes the toy and then declares "oh-oh" when no water comes out on the third and fourth squeeze. She then submerges the toy to refill it and repeats the event.

This two-year-old created her own way to document her observations of her discovery about water and the rubber toy. She used a repeated alternating pattern of two sounds, "splish-splish" followed by "oh-oh," to meter her actions. In mathematics, this doubling of the two sounds represents a model of an *AABB* pattern. Young children's activities typically reveal similar spontaneous uses of pattern thinking as they engage in activities.

A four-year-old, walking to the playground with his mother, switched from standard walking stride to a two-footed jump followed by two hops. He continued this pattern—*jump, hop, hop, jump, hop, hop*—a number of times before changing back to a walking stride.

The four-year-old was intuitively producing a pattern set of movements with an *ABB* pattern—*jump-hop-hop*. Children not only pattern activities, but they also create patterns with things that attract their attention.

> During lunch, a six-year-old silently arranged the peas on his plate into sets of two. When he reached the point where there was only one pea left, he counted each set, verified there were two in each, and ate the leftover pea. Then he smiled.

Fascination with organizing a group of peas prompted this six-year-old to partition the set of peas into equivalent subsets. He dealt with the problem of having a "remainder" by discarding it when he was unable to create one more set. His interest in having equal numbers in each group led him to get rid of the leftover unmatched pea. His smile showed his sense of accomplishment.

These vignettes vividly demonstrate that children use their own logic to generate patterns that reflect mathematical relationships in the everyday living events. Their actions are not pure imitation nor pure invention. Rather, children use what they have learned from their own experiences in ways that make sense to them. However, they can only learn the language of mathematics by listening to adults and peers (Forman & Kuschner 1977; Gesell & Ilg 1943; Vygotsky 1962; Wann 1962).

Children Progress from Intuitive to Conscious Knowing about Mathematics

Such events as the ones described above abound in the lives of children. These beginnings of mathematical thinking seem to emerge spontaneously without the children's conscious awareness of learning mathematics. With and without direct adult intervention, infants, toddlers, and young children discover and use mathematical patterns and relationships to organize their experiences. In the process of making sense out of daily experiences of using materials, participating in events, and observing and interacting with others, young children's mathematical capabilities involving number, geometry, and measurement expand dramatically.

Over the years, we have documented characteristics of the early stages of learning that shape how adults can make important contributions to children's learning (Sophian 1999). The implications of these characteristics are very compelling for adults who want to foster children's mathematical understanding and skills. They impact on how we assess what children have learned and are learning during the early childhood years so that our teaching role can make a meaningful contribution to mathematical awareness and understanding. The first two characteristics are directly linked to the emergence of language.

- Young children can often use knowledge but cannot necessarily articulate what they know. The knowledge is not yet available in a formal structure required in primary school programs. A good illustration of the existence of intuitive knowledge occurs when, after declaring that there are not enough chairs for everybody, a child is unable to explain how he or she knows. The response to the question, "How did you know that?" is, "I don't know. I just did." It is apparent that knowledge exists because the child made an accurate observation. However, the child cannot yet put this knowledge into words, and, therefore, there is little or no opportunity to extend the knowledge through discussion.
- There is a social context for learning that constitutes a critical component to the way learning is stored in the mind (Vygotsky 1962). Young children's knowledge results from a combination of independent experiences and interactions with others. They manipulate materials and talk with others about their perception of their experiences. The content of the conversations influences further explorations and discoveries about patterns and relationships within and between events. The cycle of experiences between independent learning and interaction increases in breadth and depth over time.

Implications for Teaching. In order to support the use of language to further the transformation of intuitive knowledge to the conscious knowing, it is necessary to (1) provide the language that helps children describe what they see happening and (2) elicit from them how they think about what is happening. Example: When the four-year old changed from walking to "jump-hop-hop," an adult description of the action could take the form of matching the child's action with a chant, "jump-hop-hop." The follow-up conversation about the pattern depends upon how the child responds. In another example, when the six-year-old grouped the peas two by two and ate the unmatched one, an adult comment describing what happened and asking, "Why did you eat the pea?" elicits intuitive thinking. If the child is unable to bring his thinking to a level where he can talk about it, some prompting may help—for example, "I noticed that you put the peas into groups of two and then there was one left over. Is that right?"

The second two important characteristics focus on our understanding about how children will use their growing body of mathematical knowledge; the characteristics also have implications for teaching decisions that will support owning and applying the knowledge the children are accumulating.

- Explicit knowledge gained in one context only serves when it can be generalized and transferred to contexts that vary from that of the initial learning. The purpose of counting emerges when it is used in many contexts. Its function becomes generalized as its use expands.

Implications for Teaching. Children need many opportunities to identify the mathematical relationships in differing situations. For example: After discovering that ten cookies will serve five children when each gets two cookies, further experience in distributing collections of ten builds an understanding that there will always be five groups of two items each no matter what material is used.

- Under "testing" conditions, children will often change their answers if the adult asks the same question twice, indicating a lack of a sense of autonomy in what they think they know. Without a sense of confidence or autonomy in what children think they know, they do not "own" knowledge. Confidence grows as children have the opportunity to express their ideas and exchange thinking in a context where participants respect each other (Kamii & Housman 2000).

Implications for Teaching. Support children's sharing of understanding and problem-solving strategies in situations that call for mathematical thinking and skills so that they can learn from each other. For example, engage children in collaboratively producing a project, such as re-creating the neighborhood with blocks after an exploratory walk or provide games that require computation in which children play with partners, not just opponents.

Adults Can Foster the Progression from Intuitive to Conscious Knowing

The first challenge in deciding how to provide mathematical education is to identify what children have already learned and what new understanding and skills they are generating on their own. Part of this information comes from interpreting observations of children's actions in daily events as illustrated in the opening vignettes. Additionally, children's errors provide important sources of information. These errors represent learning in process. Adults are often charmed by the errors of very young children without realizing the important ideas that are reflected in the error. For example, the comment "My mommy is older than your mommy because she's bigger" reveals a child's efforts to coordinate a relationship between observed size and a sense of elapsed time. It is considerably easier to compare size that is visible than the passage of time, which is not visible. Yet, the child's statement indicates a search to understand that relationship. Content sequences in measurement that guide how to support the growth of understanding in this area are discussed in Chapter 5.

The next challenge is to understand children's ways of learning, as discussed in Chapter 3. After we have learned what children know and can do, and we are knowledgeable about how they engage in learning, then we are in a position to make decisions about both the content and approach in our teaching role.

Finding Out What Children Know: The Content of Mathematics

One of the most important ways to discover young children's emerging mathematical skills and understanding is by watching them in action and listening to their conversation.[1] These observations of children as they pursue their own activities provide us with a window through which to see how they use mathematics as a tool in their daily living. What they know and can do is evident in all their activities. Sometimes the use of mathematical relationships is very obvious, such as when children repeatedly meter their actions with number words as they begin to count. Common chants of young children often include the number words "1, 2, 3, 4" as they pursue everyday activities like climbing and descending stairs, banging a toy, or rocking back and forth.

The younger the child, the more difficult it is to recognize mathematics in action. As they gain experience, their mathematical understanding emerges as important tools. Take, for example, the following typical interaction between four-year-olds as they jointly use a common set of materials in an activity:

> In the block corner two children were constructing their own buildings independently. The supply of some block sizes ran out as the builders added to their structures. One of the children began to collect the blocks he wanted by taking them from his peer's structure. An argument ensued:
> "Hey. Gimme my blocks back."
> "I can't. See, they belong here."
> As the argument progressed, it changed to trading blocks on a basis of one for one:
> "You give me this one and I'll give you one of mine."
> After a few trades were completed, one child again switched the negotiation to that of trading on the basis of measured lengths—two little blocks for one big one rather than one for one.

These two children initially used their existing knowledge about number in order to solve the problem of sharing resources. Their first solution after the initial "territoriality" encounter was one of numerical equivalency, exchanging blocks in one-to-one correspondence. Next, the solution changed to a consideration of length equivalency as one child realized that his building plan dictated a measured length rather than a particular number of items. Ultimately, the children found a new arena in which they began developing what bankers would call an exchange rate—one double-long block for two unit blocks or one very long block for four medium-long blocks. Mathematicians refer to this as the shifting unit.

As we reflect on the block episode, it is clear that the children are not only using mathematics to solve their immediate problem but are developing a system for exchange that goes beyond a single event. They are building the foundation for a future understanding of the base-ten exchange that defines our number system.

For more than half a century, books about young children have described the extensive repertoire of skills and the wide variety of interests they have developed during the early childhood years before school begins. Their curiosity and enthusiasm for exploring the world around them involves a pervasive use of emerging mathematics concepts and skills (Schwartz & Curcio, 1995). The most powerful context for this learning takes place when they have a high interest in what they are doing.

Instructional Planning to Support Progress in Mathematical Learning

Children learn the content and processes of mathematics in both parallel and sequential routes.[2] A *parallel route* occurs when two ideas or skills take shape simultaneously, such as sorting objects into sets and comparing the quantities of different sets. A *sequential route* occurs when new content expands existing mathematical thinking; for example, when children compute first with single-digits, and then with double-digit numbers.

Observations of children reveal whether they need to build fluency and stability (parallel learning) or whether children are ready to learn new knowledge or add new skill to their repertoire (sequential learning). Assessment as a tool for making teaching decisions is explored in Chapter 6.

Empowerment in Using Mathematics: Fluency and Ownership

A major goal of mathematics education is for young children to become fluent users of mathematics. Another major goal is for children to internalize mathematical knowledge and skills. Both early childhood educators and mathematics educators confront a similar challenge, namely, to provide progressively complex teaching and learning opportunities that help learners achieve fluency and ownership of mathematical content. Essential elements for achieving this dual goal include

- an understanding of the content or concept. For example, in space geometry, three-sided closed figures are classified as triangles, irrespective of the length of the sides and the size of the angles.

- an understanding of the big ideas that define relationships in number, geometry, and measurement, as well as data recording. For example, in the area of number, one big idea is that *the sum of two numbers is always the same irrespective of the order in which they are added* (the commutative law). Memorization of paired number facts does not necessarily include an understanding of the commutative relationship. In the area of geometry, one big idea is that *two-dimensional shapes are distinguished by the number of sides and size of angles*. Accurate labeling of a shape as a triangle or a rectangle based on memorized knowledge does not necessarily imply an understanding of the big idea.

- a facility with the necessary skills so that children can use skills effortlessly, smoothly, rapidly, and accurately.

- a sense of when and where to use the skills. This capacity constitutes ownership that occurs when learners internalize the knowledge and related skills that they can retrieve for use in a variety of situations. For example: In geometry, evidence of understanding a big idea occurs when a child declares in advance that she is going to change a rectangle made of sticks to a triangle by removing one stick and then proceeds to do it.

Instructional Issues

Scholars debate the issue of how to teach mathematics to young children. This debate evolves from three differing views of development and learning: (1) the maturationist, (2) the cognitive developmentalist or interactionist, and (3) the behaviorist (Schwartz & Robison 1982).

The maturationist view places major emphasis on children learning through play with materials and interactions with peers as they pursue activities of their own choosing. The adult role is essentially that of an orchestra director, providing materials to engage children's interests, adding experiences that relate to their interests, overseeing the social setting, and enjoying children's accomplishments with them. There is a strong emphasis on social–emotional development. Instruction features the provision of information and occurs in response to children's requests and observed needs.

The cognitive developmental or interactionist view is more carefully crafted to support children's thinking and to support emerging logic to build understanding about the patterns and relationships in their experiences. This approach also places major emphasis on children's actions and interactions with materials, peers, and adults, but the adult role is more clearly focused on supporting children's inquiry and problem solving and helping them articulate and record ideas and understandings they are generating.

The behaviorist view places primary emphasis on direct instruction followed by focused practice. Instruction is carefully sequenced in terms of difficulty. The adult role is that of transmitting the necessary information both verbally and through modeling, followed up by monitoring children's practice.

Preprimary Program Approach

Historically, most early childhood programs in the United States serving two- to six-year-olds followed the maturationist model that placed a major emphasis on action-based environments rather than traditional "lessons" (Evans 1975). From this perspective, classrooms are organized into activity centers, equipped with clusters of materials that conform to children's interests. Typically, the classrooms consist of a core of five centers: (1) blocks and block accessories, (2) art and craft materials, (3) dramatic and house play props, (4) library books and recorded tapes, and (5) construction sets and puzzles for use at tables. In addition, other choices include sand tables, water play tables, woodworking benches, and musical instruments (Hohmann & Weikart 2002). This view is supported by a large body of both theory and research about how play functions in development and learning during the early years (Fromberg 1999; Hartley, Frank, & Goldenson 1952; Van Hoorn et al. 2004). This action-based design capitalizes on the well-documented learning style that occurs during the formative years of early childhood.

The Role of Explicit Teaching. In the traditional action-based learning environment, mathematical learning flows from the children's pursuit of activities in the centers and from planned group experiences. The teaching role takes form in several of the following ways. Teachers

1. introduce mathematical experiences during group time;
2. use mathematical skills in projects and in classroom management activities;
3. provide timely support for mathematical ideas as they emerge during children's self-directed activities; and
4. provide specific materials and activities in the interest centers designed to focus children's attention on specific mathematical skills, such as counting.

Implicit Curriculum. In these action-based early childhood classrooms, the mathematics curriculum evolves when teachers observe and build upon children's interests; the curriculum is implicit rather than explicit. The mathematical learning permeates the everyday school experiences, as illustrated in the above description of the block builders. However, mathematical learning is not always identifiable, nor is it pursued within a comprehensive and cohesive design. At the same time, teachers do engage in direct instruction of some skills in order to supplement the naturally occurring mathematical learning.

The strength of this type of activity-centered program evolves from the meaningful context in which children apply their learning toward ends they value. Criticisms of this approach focus on the lack of a clearly defined, coherent mathematics curriculum.

Primary Grade Program Approach

Traditionally, primary programs serving children six to nine years of age use direct instruction as the major vehicle for mathematics education. The curriculum is explicit. Scope and sequence lists define what to teach. The format for instruction is characterized by adult transmission of content through explanations, modeling, and illustrations. Children then practice writing mathematical tasks on worksheets and in workbooks. This approach usually limits the amount of time for children to engage in activities that use the new skills in projects of high interest.

In contrast to the activity-centered approach of the preprimary program, the strength of the primary program lies in the clearly defined sequential curriculum. Critics of the structured approach focus on the lack of meaningful context for learning. They contend that the preprimary approaches do a better job of leading children to long-term use of their skills.

Building Continuity between Preprimary and Primary Programs

Over the past two decades, curriculum decisions in the field of mathematics education have increasingly merged the ideas of the action-based and structured curriculum approaches. The National Association for the Education of Young Children (NAEYC) and National Council of Teachers of Mathematics (NCTM), the leading professional organizations in their respective areas, have coordinated efforts to incorporate the strengths of preprimary and primary program designs to further public understanding about the critical elements of successful mathematics education. The impact of this collaboration has led to an increasingly more specific mathematics curriculum in the preprimary programs and the inclusion of manipulative materials for an expanded "hands-on" component in the primary programs (NCTM & NAEYC 2002).

Strengthening Mathematics Education in Early Childhood

This book is dedicated to empowering young children to understand and use mathematics as a tool in their daily lives. It is my firm belief that we can dramatically strengthen young children's mathematics learning by conceptualizing and defining an early childhood mathematics curriculum that progressively moves from concrete to abstract learning in a seamless pattern. There are four essential ingredients for successfully proceeding down the middle road between the program model dominated by the child's choice and that governed by a structured set of instructional activities that are adult scripts. A balanced mathematics education builds upon the following:

- an understanding of the critical components and sequence of ideas that define the mathematics content for the early childhood years, with sufficient detail to recognize the connection between the children's emerging ideas and the teacher's knowledge of how to match children's ideas with the next step in mathematical knowledge and skill;
- an understanding of the ways in which children collect, organize, and make sense out of their experiences;
- knowledge about the range of instructional strategies that can help young children learn mathematics; and
- a repertoire of the variety of activities that support children's acquisition and use of mathematics as a tool in life.

Concluding Remarks

The educational challenge begins with finding out what mathematical patterns and relationships children are intuitively recognizing and using. Continuity between the preprimary and primary program is shaped by children's experience and cognitive development. Strengthening mathematical learning requires integrating the use of mathematics in all kinds of activities. Chapter 2 explores the diverse ways to structure games and playful activities to support and extend children's emerging mathematic capabilities.

Notes

1. There is a wide variety of books that provide ways to observe and analyze children's understanding of their world and the skills they are using in their activities. Chapter 6 extends the discussion of assessment of children's emerging mathematical knowledge and skills.

2. The developmental sequences in mathematics for the early childhood years are discussed in Chapters 4 and 5.

References

Bredekamp, S. (Ed.). (1987). *Developmentally appropriate practice in early childhood programs serving children from birth through age eight.* Expanded ed. Washington, DC: National Association for the Education of Young Children.

Dodge, D. T., & Colker, L. (1992). *Creative curriculum for early childhood.* Washington, DC: Teaching Strategies.

Eisner, E. (1990). "The role of art and play in children's cognitive development." In Klugman, E., & Smilansky, S. (Eds.), *Children's play and learning: Perspectives and policy implications,* pp. 43–57. New York: Teachers College Press.

Elkind, D. (1986). "Formal education and early childhood education: An essential difference." *Phi Delta Kappan* 76 (7): 631–636.

Evans, E. (1975). *Contemporary influences in early childhood education.* 2nd ed. New York: Holt, Rinehart and Winston.

Forman, G., & Kuschner, D. (1977). *The child's construction of knowledge: Piaget for teaching children.* Monterey, CA: Brooks/Cole.

Fromberg, D. P. (1999). "A review of research on play." In Seefeldt, C. (Ed.), *The early childhood curriculum: Current findings in theory and practice,* 3rd ed., pp. 27–53. New York: Teachers College Press.

Gesell, A., & Ilg, F. (1943). *Infant and child in the culture of today.* New York: Harper and Bros.

Goffin, S., & Wilson, C. (2001). *Curriculum models and early childhood education: Appraising the relationship.* 2nd ed. Upper Saddle River, NJ: Prentice Hall.

Greenes, C., et al. (2003). *Navigating through problem solving and reasoning in prekindergarten-kindergarten.* Reston, VA: National Council of Teachers of Mathematics.

Hartley, R., Frank, L., & Goldenson, R. (1952). *Understanding children's play.* New York: Columbia University Press.

Hohmann, M., & Weikart, D. (1992). *Educating young children.* 2nd ed. Ypsilanti, MI: High/Scope Press.

Jones, E., & Reynolds, G. (1997). *The play's the thing: Teachers' roles in children's play.* New York: Teachers College Press.

Kamii, C., & Housman, L. (2000) *Young children reinvent arithmetic: Implications of Piaget's theory.* 2nd ed. New York: Teachers College Press.

Landreth, C. (1972). *Preschool learning and teaching.* New York: Harper and Row.

National Council of Teachers of Mathematics & National Association for the Education of Young Children. (2002). *Early childhood mathematics: Promoting good beginnings.* Washington, DC: NAEYC; Reston, VA: NCTM.

Schwartz, S. L., & Curcio, F. R. (1995). "Learning mathematics in meaningful contexts: An action-based approach in the primary grades." In National Council of Teachers of Mathematics (Ed.), *Connecting mathematics across the curriculum*, pp. 116–124. Reston, VA: NCTM.

Schwartz, S. L., & Robison, H. R. (1982). *Designing curriculum for early childhood.* Boston: Allyn and Bacon.

Segal, M., & Adcock, D. (1986). *Your child at play: Three to five years.* New York: Newmarket Press.

Sophian, C. (1999). "Children's ways of knowing: Lessons from cognitive developmental research." In Copley, J. (Ed.), *Mathematics in the early years*, pp. 11–21. Reston, VA: National Council of Teachers of Mathematics; Washington, DC: National Association for the Education of Young Children.

Van Hoorn, J., Nourot, P., Scales, B., & Alward, K. (2004). *Play at the center of the curriculum.* 3rd ed. Upper Saddle River, NJ: Prentice Hall.

Vygotsky, L. (1962). *Thought and language.* Ed. & trans. Hanfmann, E., & Vakar, G. Cambridge, MA: MIT Press.

Wann, K., Dorn, M., & Liddle, E. (1962). *Fostering intellectual development in young children.* New York: Teachers College Press.

CHAPTER 2

Designing Games and Playful Activities

Meaningful Contexts for Practice and Application

Six-year-old Maria had just acquired a new ball. Immediately she began bouncing and counting. Her counting was accurate during the first few minutes, but as she increased her control over the ball, she reached the point where her knowledge of the sequence of the counting numbers ran out "... 38, 34, 36, 37, 30, 60." Ten minutes later she was still bouncing and counting and announcing to anyone who might be listening how many times she bounced her ball without error: "I got 63." At this point, her older brother, who was nearby, declared, "Oh no. You only got 42." In response, she began again, and he joined in at the point where she lost track of the number sequence. They continued counting together for a few more minutes until she declared, "I'm hungry," and walked away.

This vignette beautifully illustrates that practice occurs spontaneously in the lives of children. Maria's attention was captured by her interest in controlling the ball as she bounced it. Counting was the tool she was using to document her increasing skill over the movement of the ball. She was practicing two skills simultaneously, the motor skill of bouncing a ball and counting the bounces to meter the action. It is interesting to note that her counting became progressively less accurate as her bouncing skill improved. It is also quite likely that, although her brother's participation improved her accuracy in counting, she did not value it at the time, because it distracted her from her primary interest, that of bouncing the ball. Nevertheless, his participation probably contributed to her awareness of the sequence of counting words.

Mathematical Fluency Develops from Speed and Accuracy

Speed and accuracy are critical dimensions of the goal of mathematical fluency. When we think about young children who are "good in mathematics," our first thought is how fast they compute. This idea is quickly followed by our expectation that they will be accurate. Ultimately, we think about the ease with which the user of mathematics selects the right tool for the task. Those youngsters whom we could describe as "not so good," because they are reluctant, insecure, or unskilled users of mathematics, tend to avoid employing mathematics as a tool in tasks. For them, rate of speed is tedious and accuracy is at risk. What the reluctant users of mathematics are missing is *fluency,* the ability to draw upon mathematical skills easily and quickly. Their use of mathematics is not sufficiently internalized nor automatically accessed.

The idea that speed increases with practice is part of conventional wisdom. However, frequency of practice is not the only criterion for success in achieving fluency. Practice needs to take place in meaningful contexts to sustain children's thoughtful involvement. *Meaningful* is a subjective term that is not easy to translate into action. What is meaningful to one individual may not be meaningful to another. Consequently, the choice of vehicles for engaging children in practice leading to the comfortable and accurate use of mathematical skills poses an ongoing challenge in reaching our goal of fluency.

Mathematical Fluency Develops through Play

Play is a primary vehicle for practice: Although play serves a number of functions in development and learning, the present focus is on the power of games and playful activities to engage and sustain children's interest in the repetitive use of mathematical skills. Our fondest hope for children is that they choose to practice targeted learnings without prompting from the adult. Choosing to practice means that the children's interest in the task maintains their involvement rather than depending upon us to keep them focused on the practice activity. There is not enough teaching time to monitor the extent of practice children need in order to develop the speed and accuracy that constitute fluency. *We need to rely upon children's interest to drive their practice.*

Games and playful activities are the contexts for practice that children choose over and over again. These contexts are universally appealing and serve to engage and sustain interested participation. Everyday observations of children remind us that repetition is a natural pattern of behavior of young children when given a material or activity that captures their attention.

Contexts for Practice

There are four major contexts for practice: (1) self-initiated and self-structured practice is the most frequently occurring context, as illustrated in Maria's ball-bouncing activity described above; (2) adult-structured and controlled playful practice such as "peek-a-boo" and "copycat" activities; (3) rule-governed games that are part of the neighborhood and school culture, such as "bingo" and bowling; and (4) written and oral drill directed by the adult. It is important to clarify the potential and limits associated with the different types of contexts for practice if we are to effectively use these different contexts as vehicles for learning.

Child-Initiated and Self-Structured Practice

Children themselves initiate and structure practice because they want to succeed in an activity. This context for practice may involve an academic skill, such as creating linear patterns on a peg board, a motor skill such as jumping rope, or a problem-solving skill such as repeatedly replacing pieces in a jigsaw puzzle starting with a different piece each time.

The *power* of self-structured practice grows out of the individual's sense of autonomy in pursuing an interest. Children feel in control and set their own standard. Curiosity often fuels their repeated attempts to achieve speed and discover possibilities.

The *limits* of self-directed practice rest in an individual's inability to recognize errors, which was evident in Maria's case, or lack of sufficient knowledge to alter strategies when they fail to achieve a desired goal, as when a child is reassembling a jigsaw puzzle and is unable to figure out why all the pieces do not fit.

We can obtain information on children's use of mathematical strategies by observing their actions and listening to their self-talk and conversations with peers. Table 2.1 provides a format for recording and analyzing observations. The first two columns specify the age of the child/children and the context of the activity and briefly describes the activity in progress. Column 3 provides space for recording observed evidence of the mathematical skills and relationships with which the child is dealing.

Table 2.1
Observing Children Spontaneously Using Mathematics

Age of Child/Children and Context	Context Activity in Progress: Materials and Actions	Talk Related to the Use of the Mathematical Skill	Mathematical Area (see code numbers below)
Example: Kindergarten child building with blocks	Makes structure with triangular-shaped blocks. Looks at structure and then selects cylinders to make towers on either side of the building. Finally, tops each cylinder with a triangular block.	Works silently. Makes intermittent nonword sounds as he places blocks—"ha," "ohhh," "there." Smiles as each section is completed.	Organizing sets using 3-D geometric blocks (1). Concern with symmetry (4) and numerical equivalency (2).
Example: Two 4-year-olds assembling a 10-piece wooden jigsaw puzzle of a truck	Each child grabs a wheel and simultaneously drops the pieces into the correct spot. One child takes the front of the truck body and experiments with fitting it onto the puzzle. The other child takes it, turns it to the correct position, and drops it in. They continue until the puzzle is complete.	The ongoing talk from the skillful child: "It goes here." "No, turn it." "See, like this." The less skillful child alternates between "No, let me do it," "Where does this go?" and "Here, you do it."	Organizing sets (1). Assembling nonstandard geometric shapes to fit together (4).
Example: Two 4-year-olds playing with sand	Two children repeatedly pour sand through funnels and sifters.	Child 1: "My sand is like water running." Child 2: "My sand is like juice running." Both children begin to laugh. "Let's make it go faster."	Using time measurement to describe observations as they experiment with properties of sand (3).

1 = Creating and organizing sets: e.g., sorting, sequencing items, building structures
2 = Comparing numerical quantity: without number, e.g., many, some; with number: counting, more–less than
3 = Use of measurement strategies: comparing length, weight, volume, time
4 = Use of geometric form: creating and comparing shapes

Column 4 provides an analysis of the child's/children's skills and understandings. This type of information-collecting helps to educate our professional eye so that we increasingly "spot" mathematics in action, and have the necessary information to plan further experiences to strengthen mathematical thinking and skills.

Adult-Designed and -Controlled Playful Activities as Practice

Adults design and control playful activities that provide opportunities to practice. Playful activities designed by an adult are distinguished from games by virtue of the fact that the adult controls the action, timing, pacing, and standards for success. For example, asking children to imitate the teacher's actions in a playful follow-the-leader format is typical of this kind of activity. There are no "published rules" that allow children to take over the activity. The actions tend to change direction to conform to adult judgments of children's needs. Typical interactions might take place during a brief waiting period when the adult initiates rhythmic clapping that children follow or during daily living activities, such as taking turns finding two socks that match when sorting the laundry. In addition to engaging children in imitation or model-copying, another form of this activity occurs when the adult copies a child's action or utterance to provoke the child's further repetition.

There are both power and limits in such playful activities. The power of playful activities rests in the adult flexibility in adapting activities to flow with the interested responses of the children. Flexible adults are sensitive to the quality of the children's responses and their involvement when picking a time or setting a pace. The limits of playful activities depend upon the adult's knowledge of the sequence of skill development and how children learn. Chapters 3, 4, and 5 elaborate in greater detail the sequence of both mathematical content and how learning progresses.

Table 2.2 provides examples of activities involving physical action, oral language, and the use of materials. It is important to note that many playful activities can attract children's interests with equal or more intensity than games because most children respond enthusiastically to the invitation to "play."

Rule-Governed Games as Practice

Practice takes place within the structure of a rule-governed game. A game is distinguished from playful practice by the public rules govern-

Table 2.2
Examples of Skill Practice in Playful Activities Shaped by the Adult

Age of Child/Children and Context	Adult-Initiated Actions	Mathematical Content
Two 4-year-olds working with pegboards	Adult sits down with own pegboard and begins to create a line of alternating red–blue pegs without talking. When the pattern takes up over half the row, the adult comments, "Look at that. I made a pattern of 'red–blue, red–blue,'" and then looks to the two children with a question, "If you were going to make a pattern, what would it be?"	Organizing sets by making a linear color pattern. The adult might also invite the children to look at her pattern and ask, "What color should I put next?" If they follow the pattern, the adult can verify, "If I do that, the pattern I started, red–blue, will continue." If they do not follow the pattern, "Oh, you want me to end the red–blue pattern and start a different one."
Small group of 5-year-olds waiting for others to come back from the bathroom.	Follow-the-leader activity using verbal directions to music. Adult: Chants the direction and follows with modeling the action: "Put your fingers on your nose, on your nose. Put your hands on your toes, on your toes. Put your hands over your head, over your head. Put your arms in back of your body, in back of your body . . ."	Locational terms of *on, on top of, over, in back of*. As children become fluent with the terms, they can take over leadership.

ing the use of the materials and the actions. For example, there are rules about how to start the game and procedures for sequence in the play of the game and how it ends. Card games, board games, tiddlywinks, pick-up sticks, beanbag toss, and bowling are typical of this class of activity. There are games that only can be played with groups, such as the "Go Fish" card game, and other games that can be played alone, such as solitaire.

The power of game-playing as a context for practice derives from the children's high interest in the "fun of the game." In group games, the other players support participation and allow players to challenge and correct each other as they take turns. The games can be designed with targeted skills embedded in the play of the game. Therefore, the focus of practice is predictable. In games with multiple players, winning or finishing the game serves as the motivation. In solitaire games, the motivation for the player is to "beat the previous score" or "complete the task of the game."

The limits of a game rest in the rigidity of the game structure. The design does not necessarily accommodate differences in skills, in personal timing and pacing, or in attitudes toward the competitive climate that accompanies a win-lose event.

Documenting Children's Use of Mathematics During Games

Watching children use the mathematical skills called forth in the scoring and playing procedures in games gives us a window through which we can assess the appropriateness of the level of skill required to succeed in playing the game. Table 2.3 is an adaptation of Table 2.1 to use for recording and analyzing children's use of mathematical skills and understandings in games. Once again, this type of information collection helps to educate our professional eye so that we will increasingly "spot" mathematics in action, and have the necessary information to adapt games and plan further experiences to strengthen mathematical thinking and skills.

Conventional Written and Oral Drill

Drill, the predominant form of practice in school programs, is characterized by oral and written repetition of what has just been taught. The most common forms of written drill practice are workbooks and worksheets as well as oral drill with flashcards or oral testing.

Table 2.3
Observing Children Using Mathematics in Games

Age of Children and Context	Game Design	Use of the Mathematical Skill	Mathematical Area
Example: Kindergarten children playing number bingo.	Individual game boards, 4 × 4 matrix, with pictured sets ranging from 3 to 8 in each box. Cue cards with numeral. Caller holds up cue card. Children cover boxes on their own board that represent the written number.	*Required*: Counting sets. *Possible extensions*: Anticipate needed numbers. Count uncovered boxes. Compare progress on different boards.	Counting and matching sets to numeral. Comparing.

The power of this approach rests in the immediate practice that follows initial instruction and, in addition, the presence of the teaching adult who can monitor the accuracy of practice.

The limits grow out of the lack of meaningful context for the children as they practice. Repeated practice in the form of isolated drill rarely sustains high interest, nor do the children connect the repetitive activity with further use. Based on our historical lack of success in producing a mathematically literate population, we are challenged to develop more effective routes for practice that assure accuracy but avoid the "math-phobic" outcomes associated with decontextualized, rote drill (Schwartz & Curcio 1995).

Each of the above contexts has value in developing children's fluency in mathematics. The choice of when to use a specific format depends upon the purpose and our knowledge of ways to capture and hold children's interest. Focused playful practice with adult participation is a viable choice when children are just beginning to use a mathematical skill. If children have learned initial mathematical understanding and skills, then games that have the targeted practice embedded in the procedures are likely to encourage children to engage in longer and more frequent periods of practice without the need of an adult presence. The section that follows examines the elements of game design that support children's independent use of the mathematical skills and understandings they are mastering.

Game Elements

Games are a part of our culture, and game playing is typically driven by personal interest. As noted above, games are uniquely suited to engaging players in repeated use of skills as a tool within the procedures that guide the players. Design formats are critical to realizing this potential.

In the world of games, there are two distinctive types: ones in which the players monitor the rules and actions, typically lotto, card, and board games, and others in which nonplayers serve a monitoring or referee function, such as in team sports of baseball and football. Almost all such games use number as part of the scoring procedure, and many involve the players in making choices that require the use of strategies that have strong links to mathematical relationships. It is important to take into consideration developmental attributes of young children along with the guidelines for sequencing both content and learning processes in order to realize the potential for meaningful practice through games. See Chapters 3, 4, and 5 for further discussion of sequences related to mathematical content and learning processes.

The Developmental Lens

It is not uncommon to hear both children and adults commenting on a game as "too easy" or "too hard." In order to design it "just right," as Goldilocks would say, we need to use a developmental lens to shape our decisions about game design and use. If children view a game as boring or incomprehensible and frustrating, they will not get actively involved and consequently the game will fail to serve its purpose.

Playful activities precede games. It is rare that preschool children, two to five years of age, have developed the necessary skills to play games with rules. Their intellectual and social development limits their ability to use their knowledge and skills in a structured game context. When we observe these young children, it becomes clear that they are beginning to find out how mathematics permeates almost everything they do. We see them engage in the following behaviors:

- They imitate others. Rote counting is typical of this kind of learning activity.
- They experiment with materials and discover relationships. Typical examples are grouping objects by color or size, lining up sticks in

size order, and organizing string beans on the dinner plate to make geometric shapes.

- They use what they know to solve problems in everyday living situations. Typical behaviors of this kind include counting cookies to assure that each person gets the same number and organizing blocks by shape as they stack them.

As we observe children in action, it is not always easy to determine whether they are *imitating, discovering,* or *using* what they know about relationships in number, geometry, and measurement. However, it is almost always clear that when they are intent on doing something, their thinking and action integrate number and action, shape and structures, and measurement relationships.

In the beginning stage of playing games, adults can begin to introduce simple action games, lotto, dominoes, board games, and card games, to children somewhere between four and six years of age. Children show that they are ready for these games by their growing interest and skill in making sets by sorting, grouping, and counting. It is important, however, to keep in mind that four- and five-year-old children are at that developmental stage in which the narrower world of games is not universally appealing. Rather, their interest plays out in a much broader field of life, as they find out about what they can do with materials and who they can control or influence and how. This means that they do not play games with the same concerns about following the rules as do older children and adults. Due to the narrow scope of games, winning and losing is not a natural concern of this age period, although they may talk about it because of ideas imposed on them by others. They do not quite understand the confines of game structures. At this age, *win* translates into "getting what I want," rather than being the first to achieve the goal of a game by following its precise rules.

The author observed a typical example of this lack of concern for game structures in a prekindergarten curriculum development project. We introduced a lotto-type game with photo copies of leaf prints made from those collected by the children on a nature walk. The game included three sizes of four differently shaped leaves. Each leaf photo was placed on one of two playing boards as well as on a card that fit the boxes on the playing boards.

The game was introduced and enthusiastically played several times with two four-year-old children in the class with adult guidance. The adult then left the children to continue on their own. The orderly structure of the game immediately disappeared. Instead of stacking the cards, drawing them one at a time, and finding the match on a playing board, the children scrambled the cards in the center of table, some with pictures showing and others not showing. Each child simultaneously grabbed a card, looked at her own board and then her classmate's board, and declared, "I got it" or "Here. This one is yours. It goes there." When there were no more cards, the conversation changed to "We're done. Wanna play again?" "Yeah. Let's play." This pattern of play continued through several rounds. When the adult returned to join them, they seemed very comfortable playing one or two more rounds in the orderly pattern of lotto. However, once again, when the adult left, they resumed using the materials as a simple matching activity without the game structure. This pattern continued with other children in the class for several weeks. For them, the game design held no meaning. They were sufficiently challenged by the matching task to pursue it and the game board served as a way for them to organize their findings. Adult temptations to ask them "Who won?" would have been totally irrelevant since that was not their concern.

As they mature in game playing, at the next stage of using game materials, children tend to focus on finishing the game based on taking turns rather than the simultaneous pursuit of the activity described above. Once again, their interest tends to be on completion, playing until there are "no more" of the resource materials, rather than quitting after one person "wins." At this stage, the standard of playing versus winning is set by the statement that, "The game is over when everybody has. . . ."

Young Children Need Choices

The competitive climate becomes more visible as children enter the first and second grade, but the developmental pace may vary as exemplified in the following observation of a six-year-old and a seven-year-old in a school's computer lab:

Two boys were playing tic-tac-toe on the computer. As they played, it was clear that the six-year-old was entranced with the process of moving the screen curser to place X's and O's on the tic-tac-toe grid, while the seven-year-old was concerned with winning the game. With each of his turns, the younger child would quickly drop an X in an empty box on the grid, without apparent consideration of the possibilities. Then he would ask his playing partner, "Where do you want your O?" In a few brief turns, the older child declared, "I win," pointing to his line of O's. The younger child would then respond, "I know. Do you want to play again?" The older child eagerly agreed.

This scenario repeated itself for almost half an hour, with both children smiling and chuckling throughout the activity. Each child was engaged in mathematical thinking but in very different realms. The younger child was fully engaged in coordinating the movement between the mouse on the horizontal plane of the desk and the cursor on the vertical plane of the screen. The older child was planning how to align a series of marks, vertically, horizontally, or diagonally. Their different perspectives did not interfere with the progress of the activity. We learn from this observation and many more like it that children vary in their interests. They need choices. They also need game-playing space to pursue what captures their attention when they are involved in the actions within games. The value each child was gaining from the experience would have been lost if an adult had sought to focus on the conventional win-lose values.

The Need to Consider Winning and Losing

The emotions that accompany both winning and losing highlight another set of needs that impel us to provide choices to children when initiating games. Winning or losing a game triggers children's ego responses and their varying abilities to deal with the ego testing.

For some children in the primary grades, stress increases as the competitive climate becomes more intense. This limits the potential contribution that games can make for these children.

Not only individual personality differences but also life's circumstances affect children's tolerances for losing. Children living in poverty and stressful home conditions often feel a loss of "control over their own destiny" (Rowe 1978). Group games in which "luck" is a major factor can produce that same sense of impotence in controlling experiences in their daily lives. In our work with children who struggle with competition in games, we have discovered that many games can be converted to solitaire formats that give children access to the fun of playing and competing with one's own record. Solitaire provides experience without the "threat" of competition and allows children to gain expertise without the debilitating force of losing.

Designing Games for Independent Play

Well-designed group and solitary games help children feel some sense of challenge as well as anticipated success. To achieve a balance between challenge and potential success, a game needs to provide a match between the children's level of mathematical understanding and the levels of the tasks embedded in a game's signal or cuing system. The balance also depends on the difficulty of the actions required of the player. Irrespective of the type of game, adults need to consider the following design elements when they create games:

- *counting*, by using dice, collecting sets, and moving a number of spaces;
- *collecting sets* based on specified criteria, such as shapes, colors, sizes, or classes of items, such as number of dogs or numbered cards;
- *symbols* to use, such as pictured sets, tally marks, or standard number notations;
- *game complexity*, such as the number of steps in a procedure, the length and shape of the game board, or the number of decisions a player would need to make; and
- *format for recording data*, such as the use of concrete drawing or writing materials.

When children beg to play a game again and again, it is a sure indicator that the design resonates with their interests and that the actions required are both challenging and doable.

Embedding Practice

When we embed skill practice in the game structure, we create the best conditions for children to practice academic skills as well as provide support for their psychomotor and social learning. Skills that are embedded do not take over the game but are integral to it. For example, in the card game of War, the comparison of number quantity determines which player will collect the two cards that are exposed. The purpose of the game is to collect cards. The procedure requires comparing the greater or lesser value of numbers.

Task Analysis

Task analysis is the process by which we assess what children need to know and are able to do in order to engage in an activity. This is the adult's critical final step in deciding to whom to offer the opportunity to play a game and if it is the right time to do so. Task analysis also contributes to an understanding of children's progress as we watch them in action. From a task analysis perspective, the ability to play War rests in the children's knowledge about the number sequence 1–10 and the increasing numerical value of these numbers. In the computer tic-tac-toe game described above, task analysis reveals that there were two major tasks involved in playing the game: coordinating movement on two different planes and thinking about the matrix. When tic-tac-toe is played with paper and pencil, only matrix thinking is necessary. Observations of differences between the game design and how the players pursue the game can inform an adult's decisions about the need to adapt a procedure (Kamii 2003).

A Philosophical Note about Game Design

We provide games for young children in order for them to become better at using the skills within the game. Games that eliminate players along the way, such as Musical Chairs, or games that end when the first player reaches the goal provide less time for participation by the least adept players. In the eyes of this author, there is little educational justification for curriculum games that provide the most practice to the most skilled, thereby increasing their advantage over the less-skilled game players. It makes more educational sense to play games in which all players have the opportunity for the practice that they need.

Criteria for Success

In addition to concerns for adapting content, conditions that govern the success of a game include how to organize materials and when to schedule activities. In essence, certain conditions are necessary to support a continuing interest during the game:

- Use materials that are attractive to children, in good condition, include sufficient number of playing pieces for the intended players, and provide for proper storage containers when not in use. Players become sidetracked if there are problems with the materials.

- Create rules and game tasks that are neither too simple nor too complex for the players' abilities. There needs to be an acceptable level of learning tension so that the players are neither bored nor unable to follow the rules. Another factor affecting the game's ability to sustain interest includes the length of waiting time, determined by the number of players and the speed with which each turn can be completed. Young children do better when the waiting time between turns is short enough that they do not lose interest.

- Provide clear and understandable procedures for playing the game. Disagreements over unclear procedures divert children's attention from playing the game.

- Allocate space and time for children to complete the game at their own pace. It is difficult for children to postpone game completion.

If these conditions are met, children can play independently, without the continuous presence of the adult. They will repeatedly use the mathematical skills embedded in the game and, in the process, gain greater speed and accuracy. Meanwhile, this frees the adult to engage in other instructional interactions where the adult presence is essential.

Cuing and Scoring Systems: Simple to Complex

Cuing systems are the spinners, cards, dice, or markers that direct the moves the players make during the game; these are the "heart and soul" of card games and board games. Scoring systems keep track of the play and document how well one plays the game. Both systems provide invaluable vehicles for embedding mathematics skill practice within the game process.

Spinners, cards, or dice serve as the primary vehicle for directing the actions of the players in board and card games. The cue may be pictures, geometric shapes, sets of dots, numerals, or any combination thereof. Adults can plan the level of difficulty to take advantage of what children know and can do. The simplest task for a player is to make an identical match with a familiar picture or a swatch of color. Geometric shapes or pictures that are less familiar provoke greater challenge. From this beginning level, the complexity increases when the following conditions are present:

1. The size of sets grows larger. As sets grow larger, the spatial arrangement usually is more varied, requiring more skill in counting.

2. The familiarity of the pictured cue decreases. In lotto games, pictures of unfamiliar objects are more difficult to match than those that are familiar.

3. Abstract symbols replace recognizable representations. The first level of abstraction is changing the cue from a picture of an object to a geometric shape. The next level introduces a written symbol, such as tallies that use an "x" and numerals to represent a quantity.

4. Computation is required. Typical examples of computation involve the use of two cues, such as adding in order to find the numerical value of two dice to determine the number of moves along a path in a board game, or as in the Double War card game in which each player adds together the value of two cards in order to determine who wins the cards.

5. There are additional signals to read in order to understand the cue. The use of three dice, two with numbers and one with plus and minus signs, requires children to figure out what form of computation is required and then to complete the computation indicated by the two numbers that are exposed.

The section that follows consists of examples of how to use the cuing system in different types of games in order to embed practice with mathematics at increasingly complex levels.

Basic Game Forms

The different game formats include games that challenge children to use a variety of cuing systems. Table games, for example, include container games, board games, and card games.

Container Games Suitable for Preprimary Children

The materials for a container game include a container and sets of objects that players compare by using one or two attributes, such as length or shape. The container may be a box or a bag; boxes are recommended because they are easier for young children to use without the help of adults. One model of a container for these activities is a box with one or two holes cut out that allow the player to take an object out of the box before seeing it.

The action in a container game can include pairs of children taking turns to draw an object out of the box. After each player removes their object, they compare and contrast the two objects in relation to an attribute such as length or shape. After deciding whether the objects are identical or how they are different, the disposition of the set is dictated by the rules of the game. For example, the rule may be: "If the sticks are the same length, one player holds them. If not, the other player keeps them," or "The holder of the longer stick keeps the set."

Note that one way to avoid the "win-lose" climate is to place two different colored mats next to the container, one marked *same* and the other marked *not the same*. The rule is to place the sets on the mats based on their decisions. The game ends when the box is empty. Children can compare the size of the collections by counting the objects on each mat.

The mathematics content in container games involves players using measurement or shape in order to compare and contrast the specific property of objects. Players also use number to document the quantity of objects in each set.

Target Games

The materials for target games such as ring toss, bowling, beanbag toss, and bull's-eye targets are typical examples of boards used for target games. Numbers on targets and the scoring process are integral components to these games.

The action in target games requires that players take a designated number of turns and keep track of their accumulated scores. Note that younger players can use chips to keep track of a score, while older players can use tally marks or numerals to compute scores.

The mathematics content of target games involves players in calculating distance, direction, and location and maintaining scoring records.

Board Games: Lotto/Bingo

Lotto/bingo is a board game of chance in which players cover squares with small markers. The materials for lotto/bingo include playing boards and sets of cards. More advanced players may also use markers and score boards. The least complex playing board is an individual board that con-

Figure 2.1.

tains a ten-box strip of squares, as presented in Figure 2.1. The next level of difficulty is a three-by-three matrix board with information entered in each box (see Figure 2.2). The largest board is usually no more that a ten-by-ten matrix. The size of the boxes ranges from two to three inches for the younger children to one to two inches in the more complex game levels.

The action in bingo/lotto requires a leader to draw a card from the top of a deck of cards and display it to the players. The player who has the matching equivalent representation on his/her board claims the card and places it on the board.

The mathematics content embedded in the cues on the simplest boards has familiar pictures and/or swatches of color in each box. The game requires the player to match one item to the same item, a one-to-one match. The complexity of the game increases with the use of geometric forms, pictured sets, and numerals. The major task for the player is to pair identical and similar cues of shapes, pictured sets, and numerals. The difference between identical and similar rests in such factors as differences in color and arrangement. For example, two red squares of the same size are identical, while two red squares of different sizes are similar. Five red dots on a card arranged differently than the one on the playing board is considered an equivalent but not an identical representation. The younger the children the more likely it is that they will not recognize equivalency, only identical representations.

Figure 2.2.

Board Games: Blank Matrix Board

Blank board games usually require players to cover squares or move markers on a board. Materials include a blank matrix board, chips or other types of markers to cover the squares on the matrix board, and dice, spinners, or cards to indicate how many squares to cover.

The action requires the players to cover squares, either in a row, a column, or a diagonal, or all of the squares. Each player takes a turn with the dice, spinner, or other cuing system and covers the number of squares indicated on the cue. The game is over when one or all players reach the goal of the game. The game can be made more complex by adding more cues, such as two cards or two dice. (See Chapter 3 for further discussion of ways to increase the complexity of a mathematical task.)

The mathematics content embedded in the cues takes the form of numbered sets or numerals that are marked on the dice, spinners, or cards. The process involves counting, adding, or identifying linear patterns. Additional mathematical content emerges as players begin to anticipate the desired amounts that they will need in order to complete a row, a column, or the whole board.

The game action may also be played in reverse. In that case, the game begins with all squares covered and the goal is to uncover all squares.

Clock-Format Board Games

Clock-format board games have the same format as lotto with clock faces. Materials include individual playing boards with clocks marked in each square. Cards with a standard analog clock face represent various clock times. The action requires players to match identical clock faces on the board with the clock face on the card.

The mathematics content is embedded in the cues when the players need to distinguish between the longer and shorter hands of the clock. The players also need to correlate the positions of each hand on the card with the numerals on the board.

In a variation for older children, materials on individual clock boards contain a movable minute hand. Cue cards are marked with time intervals, such as half hour, quarter hour, five minutes. All minute-hand markers are set at twelve.

The action requires players, in turn, to draw cards to signal how much time has elapsed between the time on the card and the time of twelve on the board. The player moves the minute hand on the board clock to reflect the time on the card clock. The goal is to move the minute hand around the board to reach twelve.

The mathematics content embedded in the cues consists of players correlating the clockwise movement of the minute hand with the time intervals designated on the cards.

Track-Format Board Games

Track-format board games reflect a variation on board games that have been described above. Materials consist of one playing board with a track, markers, and cuing tool. The simplest track has up to ten boxes in a straight line. Increasingly complex tracks have more curves and angles. Tracks may have pictures or mathematical symbols in some, or all, of the boxes.

The action in the track-format board games requires players to move markers along a track. The spinner, one or more dice, or a deck of cards provide the directions for the moves.

The mathematics content embedded in the activity is the requirement that players correlate counting with the continuous movement in a direction along a track. The simplest design uses small numbers on a straight track. Higher numbers, simple computation with two cues, and varying the direction of movement illustrate ways to add more complex mathematics content.

Design Considerations

Track Board Games

Level 1. The board is a straight path. The simplest form of a track game is a straight line, as shown in Figures 2.3 and 2.4. The starting and ending positions are clearly marked, making plain the direction of the moves. The orientation of the path is optional, vertical or horizontal, as is the direction in which the players move, from top to bottom or from left to

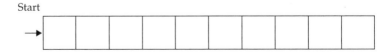

Figure 2.3. Straight Line Tracks

Start

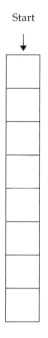

Figure 2.4. Straight Line Tracks

right. The recommended length of the track is ten to fifteen spaces that are large enough for two of the moving pieces to fit into a space, in case more than one player lands there. Young children tend to be distracted by the idea of two things occupying the same space at the same time. If illustrations are used in the spaces, they need to be small enough that they do not interfere with the space that the moving pieces will occupy between turns.

The cuing system uses single numbers between one and three that are represented by dots, stars, or another simple shape on a die, card, or spinner.

As noted above, very young children, between two and four years of age, rarely have the necessary skills to play board games. Four-year-old children usually begin to play board games. At this level, their challenge is to figure out how to continue moving in the same direction. Because the purpose of the game is unfamiliar, children can easily lose track of the direction of the movement between turns. An additional challenge grows out of their emerging understandings of "next" along the track. When moving, they usually begin the next move by counting the space the marker is occupying rather than the *next* space. The primary learning goal at this level of experience with board games is to maintain directionality. Once children are able to keep moving in the same direction they can focus on the idea of beginning to count on the space that is *next*. However direction and counting can comfortably be emphasized at the same time.

As discussed earlier, four-year-olds view the experience as an activity, rather than a game. Winners and losers are not an appropriate focus at this stage.

Level 2. A single, right-angle turn somewhere along the path, as shown in Figure 2.5, is the next level of difficulty. Once children learn to move in one direction, the next challenge is to continue in the same direction at the turning point.

The cuing system is the same as above. It is possible to try to add a number four to the cues if the track is fifteen to twenty spaces long.

It is not uncommon for young children to reverse direction at the right

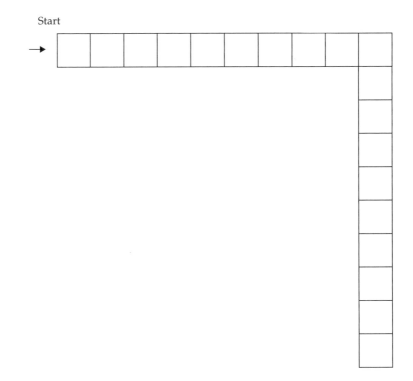

Figure 2.5. Track with One Change of Direction

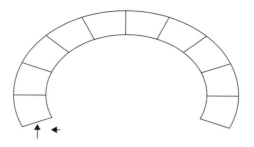

Figure 2.6. Curved Track

angle, because, once again, they fail to connect the movement along the path with the goal of reaching the end target. At this stage, they continue to focus on counting and moving, irrespective of direction. With increased experience, they may begin counting the moves using the *next* space, but we might expect that this skill will be intermittent. Again, when the end target is not a dominant concern, neither is winning. Inappropriate emphasis on "Who won?" can create confusion and diminish interest.

Level 3 and Beyond. A U-shaped track appears in Figure 2.6. A closed track, straight-line or rounded, appears in Figure 2.7. S-curve and multiple-turn tracks appear in Figures 2.8 and 2.9. As children become skilled in playing with more complex tracks, they can begin to invent game boards and develop the cues on their own. (See Table 2.4 for an overview of game formats and mathematical components. Note that the final column allows for consideration of how to reduce the level of challenge and also how to increase the degree of difficulty.)

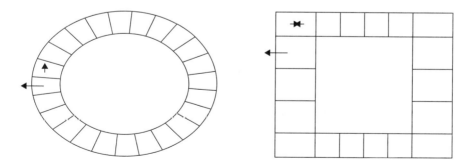

Figure 2.7. Closed Tracks: Circular and Rectangular Shapes

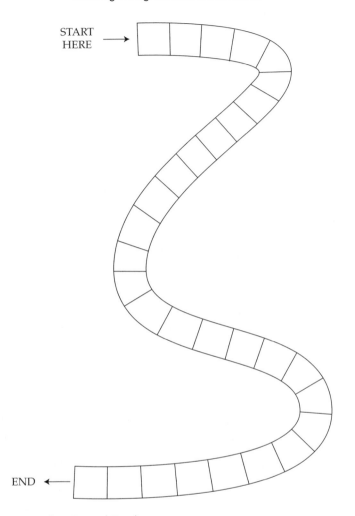

START
HERE

END

Figure 2.8. Complex Curved Track

Computation in Games

Simple computation in games can be developed within any of the formats listed above. The challenge in game design is to develop skills while allowing for adaptations in the game. In this way, it is possible to either increase or decrease the complexity of the mathematical skill while maintaining the game's momentum. Table 2.5 provides a sample of the possibilities to progress from simple to complex addition and subtraction, recording data, money coin values, and fractions in geometry.

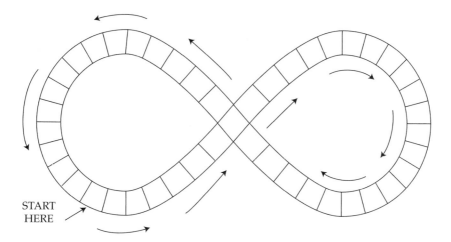

START
HERE

Figure 2.9. Path

Supervising Games

Once children learn the game, little or no adult intervention is necessary. The amount of adult supervision depends upon the classroom climate as well as the kind of game design that players find satisfying. Emphasis on prestige associated with winning, which dominates the world of competitive sports, places inappropriate demands on players of classroom games. Such competition often leads to frustration along with negative emotional and social effects.

Competition is diminished when adults help children value the process of the game. As noted above, preprimary children's notions of playing with the materials do not need, nor require, the labels of winner–loser as the prime focus of conversation about games. Primary children do care about achievement in games. Their interest can be funneled into becoming game designers. With encouragement, their interest can shift from a preoccupation with winning to the development of game adaptations that would add to the interest of the game and minimize game-playing problems.

Recognizing and addressing the causes of cheating also diminishes competition. It is important to note that "cheating" is an adult concept. Young children generally do not cheat in the sense of "planning to beat the system," unless the rewards established by the adult overshadow the activity. However, they do change rules without announcing the change

Table 2.4
Overview of Game Types and Mathematical Components

Type of Game	Decisions Involving Mathematics Components	Adjusting the Game for Increased and Decreased Difficulty

Concentration: Requires a grid for a base	Number of pairs
	Kind of pairing:
	    Identical: exactly the same
	    Similar: varying by color, size, and/or shape
	    Related: same class or group, e.g., dogs, automobiles
	Data recording procedure	

Dominoes: Matching numbers in a linear array	Pictured sets: quantity Numerals: how high? Rules for adjoining, along a line/ angles	
Card games: Creating sets, comparing sets, scoring	Sets based on pictures, symbols, numerals Identical match, similar match Size of sets Number of sets Recording scores	

Hiding games: Locating hidden objects using locational and positional cues	Terms of
	   location
	   position
	   proximity	

Physical action games:
   Target games: accumulating score
   Movement games: following verbal directions
	
	Position and location
	Direction
	Direction, location, position	

Guessing (figuring out) games: Using descriptive cues to identify an object	Size, shape, weight Set membership	
Board-track games: Moving along a track based on cues	Number, shape, direction, angles, curves Scoring procedure	

Table 2.4 (continued)

Type of Game	Decisions Involving Mathematics Components	Adjusting the Game for Increased and Decreased Difficulty
Board-lotto game: Covering boxes on lotto board based on cues	Number, shape, size 1–1 matching Scoring procedure	
Concentration: Using a base grid, locating matching sets on a grid	Number, shape, size 1–1 matching Scoring procedure Location	

and they do adapt the play of the game with or without awareness that they are doing so. If the task is too easy, they add their own twists. The changes that children make reflect a mismatch between the game design and their interests and abilities. When the task is too hard, or takes too long to complete, children will attempt to expedite the completion by skipping some of the procedures.

Children also benefit when adults recognize and respect differences in interest and ability. Differences in the abilities and interests of the players may not necessarily create conflict. The two boys playing tic-tac-toe in the earlier illustration had no problem with their different views of what was important in the game. If there had been problems, they would have called on the adult to help sort out their different perspectives and help them find a resolution. Negotiating differences that grow out of different levels of understanding is a distinctly different task than helping a child deal with such frustrations such as waiting too long for a turn or feeling that the cues were unfairly distributed. When we place too much prestige on the winning, some children will search for ways to earn that label beyond the basic game design. For example, in those games that are partially dependent upon chance, the children may see that the only recourse is to attempt to bypass chance, controlling the roll of the dice or checking the cue on cards before taking one. In these events, the adult's first concern is to adapt the game to more effectively conform with the players skills, rather than focusing on morality issues.

Once adults initiate games and activities, it is time to become the learner, that is, step back to observe children's use of the material, thereby

Table 2.5
Increasing Complexity in Computation Games

Addition and Subtraction Facts	Sample Games
	1–9 Beginning level, single digit **10–20 Next level, double digit**

Actions involve joining two numbers. Actions involve separating a set into 2 sets. Cuing materials can be:
    Two decks of numeral cards
    Pair of dice
    Two spinners
	Track board game: Use a pair of items of one cuing material, e.g., dice with sums within the target range. The sum at each turn indicates number of spaces to move a playing piece along a simple track. Goal is to reach end of track.
	Accumulation game: Use a pair of items of one cuing material to indicate how many items to take from a master set made up of such attractive materials as cotton balls or checkers or environmental objects—pine cones, rocks, shells. Goal is to acquire a designated number of objects such as 20.
	Take-away game: Each player starts with the same number of objects, and in turn, gives up number specified by the cue.
	Lotto board game: Use cards or dice. The sum of the 2 cards drawn indicates the number to cover on the playing board.

Writing Number Facts	**Sample Games**
Solitaire games: players keep a record of what happens during each turn.	Accumulation game: Have a 2-column sheet and a collection of chips. In one column record the numbers showing on each roll of the dice. In the second column, record the total amount of items accumulated. Goals: through repeated plays, find out the least number of turns required to accumulate the designated game total. Get-rid-of Game: Have a 2-column sheet, with a beginning number at the top of the holdings column. Record each roll by noting how many chips were taken away and how many are still held. Goal is, through repeated games, to find out the least number of turns required to get rid of holdings.

Table 2.5 (continued)

Money: Values of Coins	Sample Games
Equivalence: matching Exchange money for goods Activity design that involves exchanging or matching coins to obtain the same value.	Concentration game: Sets of paired cards, made up so that one card in each pair has a pictured coin, such as a dime and the other card in the set has two or more pictured coins that have the same total value as the single coin. Buying game: Two decks of cards, one with pictures of food or toys along with the value of the item, and the other with pictures of coins or a notation of money, i.e., 5 cents. Distribute 5 *money* cards to each player. Turn over 1 card from the deck of cards with the pictured items. In turn, players may buy the item or pick from the money card deck. Game goal is to buy 4 foods for a dinner plate, or fill up a 6-celled game card.
Fractions: Part-Whole Relationships Using Geometric Forms	**Sample Games**
	Concentration game: Set of paired cards that when matched create a geometric shape: circles, triangles, ovals, rectangles, squared and elongated. Go fish or rummy game: Sets of cards that require 4 parts to make a whole.

identifying their skill development and genuine interests. Watching children adapt or change rules of the game alerts teachers to the understandings and skills that children can use without help. If children simplify the game, it means they need an easier form of the game. If they shorten the game, skipping some rules, the game is too hard or too slow. If they add variations and rules, children are teaching themselves and do not need teacher intervention. Children can become game designers and in the process raise the quality of the learning for themselves and their classmates.

Concluding Remarks

Games and playful activities provide powerful vehicles to engage and sustain children's interest in using selected skills repetitively to achieve speed and accuracy. The skills are embedded in procedures and are activated in order to achieve the goals of the activity. Effective selection of the skills to embed in the games and playful activities requires consideration of the path children follow in acquiring skills and building understandings in number, geometry, and measurement. The following chapters outline the mathematics curriculum, beginning with process-product connections.

Recommended Reading

Diagram Group. (1975). *The way to play: The illustrated encyclopedia of games of the world*. New York: Paddington Press Ltd., Two Continents Publishing Group. In addition to children's party games and children's card games, the lists include (1) race board games, (2) strategic board games, (3) tile games, (4) general card games, (5) target games, (5) solitaire (patience) games, (6) dice games, (7) table games, (8) casino and gambling house card games, (9) word and picture games, and (10) games of chance.

Grunfeld, F. (Ed.). (1975). *Games of the world: How to make them. How to play them. How they came to be*. New York: Holt, Rinehart and Winston. Includes detailed descriptions and illustrations of traditional games from different cultures, many of which have become part of the American game repertoire.

Kamii, C., & Housman, L. (2000). *Young children reinvent arithmetic*. 2nd ed. New York: Teachers College Press. Two of the chapters feature games that served as core activities for practicing mathematical skills and extending mathematical thinking in first grade. Chapter 10 describes "games involving logic, reasoning, small numbers and numerals." Chapter 11 is devoted to "Games involving Addition and Subtraction."

Kamii, C., & Joseph, L. (1982). *Number in preschool and kindergarten*. Washington, DC: National Association for the Education of Young Children. The theme of Kamii's work is that mathematical thinking is an ongoing process with children and that we can capture that thinking energy through activities that conform with children's interests and level of understanding. One major route for engaging children is through games. The last section of the book (pp. 52–68) provides a variety of game designs in the following categories: aiming games (task is to hit a target), hiding games, races and chasing games, a guessing game using numerals (task is to guess whether a hidden numeral is more or less than the exposed numeral), board games, and card games.

Kamii, C., & Joseph, L. (2004). *Young children continue to reinvent arithmetic—2nd grade: Implications of piaget's theory*. Chapter 8, "Group Games," includes games involving addition using sit-down formats with such materials as cards, track boards and playing boards, dominoes and domino-type materials, puzzles, and peg boards. Physical knowledge activities (physical action) include throwing games, such as ring toss, games using a stick to hit an object, games dropping an object, leverage games, such as tidily winks, and games involving money. Computation is an essential ingredient in the games. In addition, this section describes games designed by children.

McConville, R. (1974). *The history of board games.* Palo Alto, CA: Creative Publications. Includes game-board diagrams and instructions for more than sixty games. Permission is given to teachers to reproduce up to fifty copies of any part of the book for classroom use.

Millman, J., & Behrmann, P. (1979). *Parents as playmates: A games approach to the pre-school years.* New York: Human Sciences Press. Offers a large variety of "playful approaches to activities" with young children, many of which involve mathematical ideas, skills, and content.

Nuffield Mathematics Project. (1967). *I do and I understand; Beginnings; Mathematics begins pictorial representation; Mathematics in the first three years; Shape and size.* A series of books published as a part of the Nuffield Mathematics Project developed in England during the 1960s. The books provide many descriptions of high interest activities for children in which mathematics is deeply embedded. There are many photographs of children's work along with the presentation of curriculum possibilities. While limited in game designs, many of the playful activities have great potential to develop further.

Wakefield, A. (1998). *Early childhood number games: Teachers reinvent math instruction.* Boston: Allyn and Bacon. Four of the seven chapters are devoted to describing games, many of which are accompanied by game boards and illustration of props. Chapter 3 deals with "cover-up" games. Chapter 4 features games using money. Chapter 5 describes games for the outdoors, and Chapter 6 draws on stories in children's literature to shape games.

References

Kamii, C. (2003). "Modifying a board game to foster kindergarteners' logico-mathematical thinking." *Young Children* 58 (September): 20–26.

Rowe, M. (1978). *Teaching science as continuous inquiry.* 2nd ed. New York: Holt, Rinehart and Winston.

Schwartz, S. L., & Curcio, F. R. (1995). "Learning mathematics in meaningful contexts: An action-based approach in the primary grades." In *Connecting mathematics across the curriculum*, pp. 116–124. Reston, VA: NCTM Yearbook.

CHAPTER 3

How Young Children Learn Mathematics

Content and Process Connections

A three-year-old child was walking across the room carrying a long block and repeating softly, "Ohhh. Ohhh." His body language, a bent-over position, indicated his perception of the weight of the block. As he passed by the teacher, she said, "It is heavy, isn't it?" Without stopping, the child continued on his way, repeating, "Yeah. Heavy. Heavy. Heavy," and added the motion of slowly raising and lowering the block.

Young children learn mathematics when there is a match between how they learn mathematical content and how adults help them to learn the content. In the vignette, the timeliness of the teacher's introduction of the language label *heavy* accounts for the speed with which the child added oral language to accompany his nonverbal actions. The language further helped him to extend his growing understanding of weight, as evidenced by the additional movement of raising and lowering the block. The teacher's response resulted from a coordination of the information she gained through observing with her knowledge of how thinking about measurement develops from intuitive knowing to conscious knowing. The child increased his knowledge about weight as a property of an object through the action of transporting the block. In this event, the process of learning and the mathematical content were almost inseparable because the child had a direct experience with weight.

In effect, the teacher knew that language, acquired in a meaningful context, sets the stage for conversation that can further the movement along the path from intuitive to conscious knowledge. Although the three-year-old quickly incorporated the word "heavy" to accompany his actions, it is not likely that he would be able to talk about the concept of *heavy* in situations that were very different, such as talking about comparing the weight of two different objects. He will need many more experiences that coordinate the label of *heavy* with other materials before he becomes able to discuss comparative weights.

The interdependence between content and process has captured major educational attention over the past few decades. When children's learning processes are active, the children acquire content that is integral to the activity. It follows that when adults provide mathematical content in active forms the children's mathematical learning processes are active.

It is interesting to note that professionals in the fields of both early childhood and mathematics education agree on the importance of both content and process, although their position statements have a slightly different emphasis:

National Association for the Education of Young Children	National Council of Teachers of Mathematics
The Process	*The Content*
The goal of the math[ematics] program is to enable children to use math[ematics] through exploration, discovery and solving meaningful problems. (Bredekamp 1987, p. 71)	The curriculum is mathematically rich . . . [with] concepts and procedures. . . . [It provides] a common foundation of mathematics to be learned by all students. (NCTM 2000, pp. 3–5)

There is a clear consensus that effective curriculum requires the coordination of mathematics content with an understanding of the inquiry processes children use to develop mathematical understandings. NAEYC places emphasis on how children explore, make discoveries, and solve meaningful problems. NCTM places emphasis on what children learn when they explore, discover, and apply their understandings to solve problems. The recognition of the rules that govern how children acquire information and organize it shapes adult decisions about how to select materials, and design activities and interactions.

How Young Children Learn Mathematics: The Beginnings

Young children learn about the content and process of mathematical learning long before adults launch instruction through a planned curriculum. Initial discoveries from infancy onward serve as the seeds for the development of an organized set of understandings. As discussed in Chapter 1, knowledge initially takes form at the *intuitive* rather than the *conscious* level of awareness. Thinking about time measurement begins for a crying infant with an awareness of the connection between the appearance of the adult and the reduction in discomfort, through food, diaper change, or other forms of human comfort. As a sense of time develops, the sound of the approaching adult informs the infant that "help is on the way" and the crying ceases in anticipation of the arrival of the adult. Similarly, distance measurement and locational thinking are provoked as infants reach for hanging toys in their cribs.

Toddlers make further connections within events related to their own actions as well as with others. When they stack a few blocks, the stack is stable; when they stack a lot of blocks, the stack falls. When they blow a bubble in the bathtub, it "flies away" and at some distance it bursts. When they try to catch it, they are figuring out the direction and speed of movement.

Experience provokes awareness of similarities and differences and patterns and relationships in such mathematical components as quantity, shape, size, location and position in space, and direction and speed of movement. Over time, infants, toddlers, and young children begin to see patterns in the events shaping their expectations and actions. As they acquire language, their initial discoveries eventually become sufficiently familiar that they can talk about their expectations and new discoveries. At this point, their emerging understandings begin to enter the conscious level of knowing, as exemplified in the following vignette.

A three-year-old was silently changing the shape of a ball of clay by rolling it back and forth, making it thinner and longer with each roll. While he worked, he spoke quietly to himself, saying, "I'm making a snake." In fascination, he watched as the length of the snake increased. When the snake was about two feet long, he changed his action from rolling to stroking, placing both hands at the center and slowly moving them along the snake to the ends. As he repeated this stroking, he began to quietly chant, "long, long, long."

Shape and measurement captured the attention of this three-year-old. At first, the child was completely engaged in changing the shape of the clay from a spherical to a cylindrical form and then increasing the length of the cylinder. His self-talk revealed his growing awareness of the changes he was making as the snake got longer, culminating in the declaration of *long*. His process was clear. He was using multiple senses—he looked at the clay, he rolled it, he stroked it. What is not so evident is the fact that his use of the term "long" revealed an emerging concept about length as a *comparative* rather than an *absolute* property of the object. He was dealing with content by comparing what he saw at the moment— "long"—with an idea of "not long" that was in his head. The idea of "not long" was fed by his mental image of what it looked like when he began rolling clay. A critical dimension of mathematical content in measurement is the comparative element. No object is *long*. Rather is it longer or shorter than another object that is either visible or mentally imagined. Similarly, children eventually understand the comparative rather than absolute aspect of measurement by experiencing the measurement dimensions that precede the use of measurement tools, such as weight, or temperature, or speed. The three-year-old child is entering that stage where conversation about comparative length can support the movement from intuitive to conscious knowing about relative measurements.

How Adults Help Young Children Learn Mathematics: The Beginnings of Curriculum

The interaction between the teacher and a three-year-old carrying the block illustrates an initial stage of curriculum. The teacher's statement, "It is heavy," provided the child with the language to talk about his perception of weight. In order to "teach," we need to find ways to advance intuitive knowledge so that it is accessible for children to talk about it. (Chapters 6 and 7 explore the range of instructional strategies for planning, assessing and communicating with children.)

However, before making the selection of how to teach, we need to consider the path along which mathematical learning moves from both the process and content perspective. Curriculum begins when adults interact with children to stimulate, inform, extend their thinking, and challenge them to think about new ideas. Adults select strategies for instruction on the basis of the function that they intend the strategy to serve. For example, if the function is to introduce new possibilities, the adult takes the role of information-giver. If, on the other hand, the function is to provoke discovery of new possibilities, the adult role is one of raising questions.

The Context for the Beginnings of the Mathematics Curriculum

It is apparent that the major portion of young children's learning occurs in action-based activities. The younger the children, the more they depend upon all of their senses for collecting information to feed their thinking. The building of initial understanding flows from looking and listening, touching and manipulating, lifting and dropping, pushing and pulling, jumping, climbing, and running. As they engage in these active inquiry processes, mathematics understanding and skills in number, geometry, and measurement serve as part of the tools for accumulating and organizing information. Young children's actions and interactions with others contribute to their mathematical learning. Adults tend to think of this active learning pattern as *play*.

Play: A Primary Vehicle for Learning Mathematics

A great deal has been written about the meaning of play and how it propels learning during the early years (Fromberg & Bergen 1998; Klugman & Smilansky 1990; Monighan-Nourot et al. 2004). Adults who are inexperienced at working in action-based environments tend to view play as what occurs in between the periods of formal instruction that follows a curriculum plan. In our adult world, we view play as the counterpart of work. For us, work constitutes focused and product-oriented behavior, requiring self-discipline and the avoidance of distractions. Adult play serves as a release from externally imposed tasks.

Children at play demonstrate many of the qualities ascribed to adult work. They are fully engaged, focused, and outcome-oriented. We can see this when they are engaging in the following activities:

1. Finding out about such events as how water splashes when they drop it from a height or what shapes appear when they bend a pipe cleaner. For the child the outcome is the information she/he collects through exploration. Negative adult views of this behavior are best illustrated by the terms "playing around" or "fooling around."

2. Using what they know to solve problems in the process of accomplishing a goal or producing a product, such as successfully stacking a set of blocks or creating a basket with art materials. For the child, the outcome is the product that results from thoughtful ma-

nipulation of materials or a planned arrangement of objects to produce a particular effect. Adults frequently view this type of activity as "entertainment, not learning."

3. Interacting with others by sharing observations with peers and adults or solving problems that occur during activities. For the child, the outcome is an exchange of perceptions and ideas to further the activity in progress. Adults tend to view children's interactions as "just" social conversation.

4. Playing games that are in the popular culture. The adult value of game-playing by children usually reflects the competitive perspective. Winning, to adults, is often the most important outcome.

Decades of study about the self-directed activities of preprimary children reveal the extensive amount of mathematical learning that occurs as they play. This early mathematical learning serves as an essential foundation for more formalized instruction. Curriculum is born when we organize the environment and interact with children as they play (Dittman 1970).

The Need for a Curriculum Map

Programs in which play and self-directed activities constitute the core of the program are designed to capitalize on children's keen interest in exploring the environment, manipulating, constructing, experimenting with materials, and interacting with others. These programs place high value on the following skills that children demonstrate:

- Inquiry skills are apparent as they accumulate information from their actions and interactions, and

- Organizational skills are evident as children collect information, make connections that generate concepts and understandings, and see patterns and relationships.

In child-centered programs, adult input takes place in order to provoke increasingly complex thinking about actions and interactions. Adults select and arrange materials and activities in order to add curriculum content. Adults face the challenge of selecting the sequence of mathematical content and learning processes that define how children progress from novice to expert in their understanding and use of mathematics. This requires a map of the route that defines the important or critical stages in the learning of mathematics, one that becomes a map in our heads for use in guiding our instructional decisions.

In the everyday life of childhood in school and out, many opportunities arise for the adult to contribute to children's developing mathematical understanding. However, without a curriculum map of the key processes and content elements that govern learning, it is difficult to make a selection from the various possibilities. The choice of the most effective instructional strategy flows from knowledge about how children access and organize knowledge as well as the content that children need to learn.

There are some generic rules about learning processes that are accepted by each of the major approaches to learning and that define instructional direction. Understanding the rules that define how the learner processes content guides the design of the activities and adult interactions.

Rules to Sequence the Development of Mathematical Knowledge

The following rules are divided into two sets. The first set follows the route from the initial acquisition of information to understanding. It deals with how children's minds process information. The second set describes the way children acquire information that they process. Just as the information path to concept development follows a predictable path, so, too, do the strategies that children use in order to collect information.

The following four rules, or guidelines, define the sequential, generic path for processing information:

1. Young children move from concrete, to representational, and then to abstract thinking. Children initially discover relationships between materials and events in the three-dimensional world. Concrete materials serve as the central tool for children to think about objects, actions, and events. Pictures and symbols take the place of concrete objects only after children have built a foundation through sufficient direct experience. Over time, mental images emerge for children to use as a reference for direct experience.

2. Children's initial understanding of mathematical sets grows out of their early experiences as they make collections of concrete materials to serve their own purposes. The ability to represent a collection in pictures depends upon their ability to transform images from

the three-dimensional world of things to two-dimensional surfaces. Ultimately, the ability to think about patterns, numerical quantity, or geometric form depends on the images that children have constructed in their minds. We often can see this full range of development when working with a group of primary-age children engaged in solving word problems. Some use blocks to illustrate the problem, others draw pictures or write tally marks, while still others complete the computation in their heads. This diversity reflects the need to provide materials for those children who are working their way along the path from concrete to abstract thinking (Carpenter et al. 1999; Copley 2000; Dutton & Dutton 1991; Kamii & Joseph 1982; Whitin, Mills, & O'Keefe 1990).

3. Children's learning progresses from the known to the unknown. When meeting something new and unfamiliar, the mind automatically compares the new object, physical experience, or idea with prior understanding. Psychologist Lev Vygotsky describes this learning process as a *Zone of Proximal Development* in which the learner makes sense of new learning by closely associating it with what the learner already knows (Moll 1990). Epistemologist Jean Piaget refers to this process as *equilibration*, the mechanism by which the mind seeks a balance between taking in new knowledge that fits what is known and readjusting generalizations to make room for an unfamiliar idea (Lavatelli 1970). Behaviorists refer to this process of connecting learning as "incremental learning," adding new information and expanding skills in closely related increments (Skinner 1979). This guideline links closely to the one above in the sense that the emerging mathematician begins to learn from the most familiar content in the concrete world of things. In learning mathematics, young children demonstrate this process of moving from the known to the unknown when they convert a computational problem to number combinations with which they are familiar. For example, in a word problem that requires mentally adding 9 and 15, some children will edit the problem by using familiar combinations, such as "10 and 15 make 25, so 9 and 15 make 24." In this instance they have used what they know as a jumping-off point for solving an unfamiliar problem (Kamii & Housman 2000; Carpenter et al. 2000). Younger children demonstrate this sequence rule when they separate cookies into groups of two in order to find out how many they need in order to distribute two to each child sitting at their table.

4. Children learn mathematics from simple to complex knowledge and skills. Simple learning situations have fewer variables—a fewer number of items—thereby presenting children with fewer choices. However, it is important to realize that if there are *no* choices, thinking is not likely to take place. Dealing with more complex situations requires an ability to see patterns and relationships and helps children to make informed choices from a wider array of possibilities. In mathematics learning, when children develop competence in creating linear patterns, the simplest task is to copy a pattern from a model, for example, creating a red–blue poker chip pattern. A more complex task is to create a single alternation pattern with materials of one's own choosing, such as a "heart–flower" pattern for a greeting card or placemat. The simplest form to figure out a word problem is to complete one computation, as illustrated in the following addition, or joining, problem: "Jim had two marbles and his friend gave him three more. How many does he now have?" The more complex level requires two steps in the computation. "Jim had two marbles. One friend gave him two more and another friend gave him three more. How many does he have now?"

The following three rules define the progression of learning strategies that children use as they collect information:

1. Children find out about new ideas by moving from exploration to experimentation. Children initially learn through their senses in the world of concrete objects. Direct experiences serve as the foundation for abstractions. Then children use stored mental images of objects and events to propel their experimentation and feed predictions. In mathematics, when adults present a new collection of materials, children's natural curiosity leads them to manipulate the objects in a variety of ways to discover more about them. The mathematical properties—shape, size, and weight—are major factors of such exploration. After the children's initial identification of some attributes of the object, the next phase is to experiment with the object, such as by setting objects into motion to ascertain how they move. The difference in movement between rectangular solids and spheres sparks an understanding of the unique attributes of shapes with straight edges and rounded surfaces. This information, in turn, can shape the way children perceive a sorting task that eventually can lead to their

comparing the size of sets. At a next stage, experimenting with ways to group and regroup a set with a given number of objects leads to the ability to hypothesize on how many equivalent groups can be formed. Children need to understand about how many equivalent groups are possible in order to distribute materials equally.

2. Children develop beyond imitating or copying to replicating from memory to creating new ideas. When children replicate images from their memory, it is similar to envisioning pictures, although the pictures are in their heads rather than on paper. The ability to transform a picture in the mind, to apply the idea to another kind of situation, grows out of an abstraction of the idea. In mathematics, children begin to imitate counting as they observe others use the counting words. After considerable repetition of this rote recitation of the number words, they memorize the list of numbers in the same way that children memorize nursery rhymes (Schwartz & Robison 1982). Rational counting or meaningful counting begins to take form as children imitate not only the word sequences but also the actions that accompany the listing of the number words. Subsequently, children repeat the word list along with the actions even though the model is no longer present. In time, the imitated activity takes on meaning and leads to meaningful, rational counting. This guideline also links with the progression of concrete to abstract. Imitating is bedded in the concrete, as the child copies what is visible.

3. A first step toward developing concepts is to accumulate facts. Multiple related experiences add to the child's accumulation of facts. In turn, the child integrates related experiences in her/his mind during the process of building concepts. In mathematics, children first learn the fact that a three-sided plane geometric figure, such as an equilateral triangle, is called a triangle. They also learn the fact that a slightly different shape, perhaps an isosceles triangle, also is called a triangle. Multiple experiences with different representations of triangles in a variety of sizes leads to the collection of facts that feed a developing concept about common properties of triangles, a closed figure with three sides and three angles. In terms of three-dimensional objects, children first learn that standard-shaped balls vary in size. Multiple experiences with spherical objects help children to discriminate between a conventional ball and oval-shaped spheres.

It is important to note that all thinking strategies lead to "knowing" and that children use knowledge, with increasing accuracy over a period of time. In the process of solving problems, children adapt and refine their knowledge.

Tables 3.1 and 3.2 define and illustrate the application of these sequencing rules in curriculum planning and in management activities. Table 3.1 defines a sequence for developing linear patterning activities. The progression moves from a single alternation of two discrete sets of material, defined by mathematicians as AB pattern. The challenge in-

Table 3.1
Sample Sequence for Developing Linear Patterning Activities

This example uses the following rules:
  Simple to complex: increasing the number of variables, number of items, and differences in the variables
  Copying to creating: from direct copying to copying from memory to creating
  Concrete to abstract: from object model to picture model

Level of Difficulty	Task
1. Copy a model exactly. Simplest pattern: AB—single alternation pattern with 2 sets of concrete materials.	Using 1 set of tongue depressors and 1 set of cotton balls; pattern: stick, ball, stick, ball, repeated 3 times.

2. Increase complexity.
• The size of the unit becomes larger
  AABB—double alternation
  ABCB
	Copy: stick, stick, ball, ball (AABB)
	Copy: big stick, ball, little stick, ball (ABCB)

• The distance between model and task area lengthens • The length of the pattern increases	Place the model at one end of the table and work space at other end. Repeat pattern 5 or 6 times.
3. Change the task from copying the pattern to extending the pattern. AABBAABB_____ Fill in the missing items: AABBAABBA__BBAA__B	Given a pattern with unit repeated twice, extend the pattern. Fill in the missing item(s) in a pattern that has been repeated twice.
4. Create a pattern and label the unit.	In craft activities, create a pattern, repeat it several times, and label the pattern, e.g., a red, red, blue pattern.

Table 3.2
Sample Sequence for *Creating and Organizing Set* in Preparation for Lunch

---

This example uses the rule of moving from simple to complex by (1) increasing the number of items in the set, and (2) changing the task from direct copying to copying from memory.[1]

Initial level:
Distribute 1 item to each child, such as a cup to each of 2–4 children at one table **after** teacher models the procedure using napkins.

2nd level:
Increase the number of items **or** the number of children.
  Task: Serve 1 item to two tables, 10–12 children.
  Task: Serve 2 items to 1 table, such as napkins and cups for 6 children.

3rd level:
Increase the number of items in set.
  Task: Create a set for each child, such as plate, napkin and utensils.

4th level:
Create an ordered set.
  Task: Place each item in the set in a specific position initially by copying the model and then reproducing it from memory.

---

1. Adapted from S. Schwartz & H. Robison (1982). *Designing curriculum for early childhood* (Boston: Allyn and Bacon), p. 74.

creases when the pattern gets longer, AABB, and even more so with an AAB pattern.

At the next level of development, children extend the length of a pre-existing pattern. In order to do this, they must be able to recognize the repeated unit in order to continue it. Finally, when children create a pattern, based upon their ability to recall possibilities, they need to decide what the pattern unit will be and how many times to repeat it.

Children can use the sample sequence shown in Table 3.2 when they prepare the table for lunch; they have to create and organize a set of items. Here they need to focus on spatial organization, rather than on a linear pattern. Again, at the first level of development, children copy a visible model. At the next level, children replicate a model that exists as a picture in their minds, a mental image.

Concluding Remarks

The recognition of the rules that govern how children acquire and organize information and develop mathematical understanding helps adults to select materials and design activities and interactions. Adults who apply these rules to the mathematics curriculum also require a map of the mathematical content sequence. Chapters 4 and 5 deal with content maps for number, geometry, and measurement.

There are rules governing the way children learn mathematics content and skills. These rules guide the development of curriculum. The next chapter defines the content for curriculum in the area of number.

References

Bredekamp, S. (Ed.). (1987). *Developmentally appropriate practice in early childhood programs serving children from birth through age 8.* Washington, DC: National Association for the Education of Young Children.

Carpenter, T., Fennema, E., Franke, M., Levi, L., & Empson, S. (1999). *Children's mathematics: Cognitively guided instruction.* Portsmouth, NH: Heinemann.

Copley, J. (2000). *The young child and mathematics.* Washington, DC: National Association for the Education of Young Children; Reston, VA: National Council of Teachers of Mathematics.

Dittmann, L. (Ed.). (1970). *Curriculum is what happens.* Washington, DC: National Association for the Education of Young Children.

Dutton, W., & Dutton, A. (1991). *Mathematics children use and understand: Preschool through third grade.* Mountainview, CA: Mayfield Publishing Co.

Forman, G. E., & Kuschner, D. S. (1983). *The child's construction of knowledge: Piaget for teaching children.* Washington, DC: National Association for the Education of Young Children.

Fromberg, D. P. (1999). "Play." In Seefeldt, C. (Ed.), *The early childhood curriculum: A review of current research,* pp. 35–74. New York: Teachers College Press.

Fromberg, D. P., & Bergen, D. M. (Eds.). (1998). *Play from birth to twelve and beyond.* New York: Garland.

Harlen, W. (2001). *Primary science: Taking the plunge.* 2nd ed. Portsmouth, NH: Heinemann.

Hartley, R., Frank, L., & Goldenson, R. (1952). *Understanding children's play.* New York: Columbia University Press.

Kamii, C., & Housman, L. (2000). *Young children reinvent arithmetic: Implications of Piaget's theory,* Chapter 4, pp. 75–65. 2nd ed. New York: Teachers College Press.

Kamii, C., & Joseph, L. (1982). *Number in preschool and kindergarten: Educational implications of Piaget's theory.* Washington, DC: National Association for the Education of Young Children.

Klugman, E., & Smilansky, S. (Eds.). (1990). *Children's play and learning: Perspectives and policy implications.* New York: Teachers College Press.

Lavatelli, C. (1970). *Piaget's theory applied to an early childhood curriculum.* Boston: Center for Media Development, Inc.; American Science and Engineering, Inc.

Moll, L. (Ed.). (1990). *Vygotsky and education: Instructional implications and applications of sociohistorical psychology.* Cambridge: Cambridge University Press.

Monighan-Nourot, P., Scales, B., & Van Hoorn, J., with Almy, M. (2004). *Looking at children's play: A bridge between theory and practice.* New York: Teachers College Press.

National Council of Teachers of Mathematics (NCTM). (2000). *Principles and standards for school mathematics.* Reston, VA: NCTM.

Schwartz, S. L., & Robison, H. F. (1982). *Designing curriculum for early childhood.* Boston: Allyn and Bacon.

Skinner, B. F. (1979). *The shaping of a behaviorist.* New York: Alfred A. Knopf.

Whitin, D., Mills, H., & O'Keefe, T. (1990). *Living and learning mathematics: Stories and strategies for supporting mathematical literacy.* Portsmouth, NH: Heinemann.

CHAPTER 4

How Young Children Learn
Number Concepts and Skills

The teacher's role is to know where a child is in his thinking and to help him to extend his knowledge and to make it more meaningful. She must understand the beginnings of the key concepts and in turn must supply the keys which are door openers for thinking about a set of phenomena or a group of ideas. —K. Wann, M. Dorn, and E. Liddle, *Fostering Intellectual Development in Young Children* (1962)

A curriculum map drawing landmarks along the path of young children's development of number concepts and skills outlines a reasonable range adults can follow to sequence their instruction of, and support for, children's learning. Such a map identifies the big ideas that constitute learning along the route, thereby illuminating possibilities of the different ways in which the big ideas for teaching take shape in action. The map not only defines the major understandings that young children can build but also the range of skills that support the growth of these understandings. It provides the landscape for identifying the mathematics that children are using. Our recognition of the many faces of the big ideas as they emerge in activities of young children shapes decisions on how to nourish the ongoing mathematical learning. Adults who are well-informed about how children learn are in the best position to shape conversations with children that have the greatest potential to enrich children's understandings about the mathematical relationships embedded in their daily activities (Bredekamp 1987; Doverborg & Samuelson 2000; Greenberg 1984; Kamii and Joseph 1982; Monighan-Nourot 2004).

The content maps described below outline key ideas that can help children to develop their number concepts. The maps also distinguish between key ideas that children can learn simultaneously and those ideas that develop in a sequential order. Examples are provided in the next section to illustrate the ideas and illuminate further possibilities.

The first map is an overview of the stages by which young children progress from early experiences with sets—grouping and sorting objects—to computations that include double-digit numbers (see Table 4.1). The big ideas are generic and indicate the sequence in which they are most likely to develop. From top to bottom, the map defines those understandings that develop before counting as Level 1. Children develop their foundation for counting by creating and organizing sets with concrete materials. At the same time, they are developing an awareness of the quantitative properties of a set as well as its other properties. At Level 2, children develop an emerging sense of number while they acquire beginning counting skills. At this stage, children discover the relationship of number to set, and the various ways that regrouping affects numerical quantity. Level 3 deals with computation, first with single-digit and then double-digit numbers. The distinct factors that affect the complexity of a computation problem are discussed in this section.

In essence, the three critical stages identified span mathematical number learning from (1) the initial development of concepts of sets in the world of things, through (2) counting and the emerging number sense, and then (3) beginning computation. Each stage or level involves an array of integrated learnings that establish the foundations for the next stage.

Skills before Counting

Two kinds of understandings need to develop before children engage in rational counting in order to discover the meaning of numerical quantity: the development of concepts of set which serve as the focus of counting, and the subskills that children use in the process of rational counting, or counting to quantify a set.

Concepts of Set

Children develop their understandings about sets as they use materials, produce actions and sounds, and participate in events. Knowing how children make progress in thinking about sets helps adults recognize

Table 4.1
Curriculum Map: Developing Number Sense

Level 1: Prenumber

Creating Sets	Comparing Quantities of Sets	Organizing Sets
Big ideas: *Sets can be created for various reasons.* *Sets can be matched, item-to-item, across sets.* Classifying Sorting Pairing and clustering	Big ideas: *Sets can be compared using non-numerical quantifiers such as "more," "a lot."*	Big ideas: *Sets can be organized in different ways:* *by creating subsets* *by creating patterns*

Familiarity with number words in sequence (rote counting) also develops during this period.

Level 2: Discovering Number Meanings

Counting
Big ideas: *Numerical quantity is defined by counting.* *Numerical quantity does not change with the order of the objects in the set.* *An empty set is a set with no members.*

Level 3: Computation

Computation with Single-Digit Numbers	Computation with Double-Digit Numbers
Big ideas: *A set can be described quantitatively in more than one way.* *Numerical patterns and relationships can be described.*	Big ideas: *Equivalency can be retained when shifting units.* *There are multiple ways to compute accurately.*

timely moments to refine classification thinking and provoke interest in counting sets. The following summary of the stages are abstracted from the work of Kofsky (1966):

Clustering. Very young children initially group objects in terms of their personal experiences rather than the objective properties of the objects. For example, they may make a collection of objects that appeal to them, such as a piece of cotton, a stick, or a candy wrapper. Adults may tend to view this kind of activity as unimportant because the reasons for the cluster are clearer to the child than to the observer. It is important to consider these experiences as the precursor to traditional sorting. If the child can understand the language, some conversation about the collection with an adult can move the child's thinking from the intuitive to the conscious level.

Pairing. Pairing is the first level of sorting. Paired objects, such as shoes, mittens, arms, and ears, pervade children's lives. In turn, children create their own pairs as they manipulate and dramatize with play materials. Common examples include pairing miniature trucks, or pairing two toys that go together, such as one truck with one "driver."

Sorting. The progression from simple matching to consistent sorting occurs as children group objects and make decisions about which items belong to a group and which do not. It is easy to be misled about children's sorting abilities if we are not aware of how the type of collection affects children's interest. In addition to interest level, provision of very large collections that offer too many possibilities may falsely suggest that the child cannot sort. Involvement in counting is most likely to occur during this sorting period.

Classifying. Classification involves identifying functional similarities or essential patterns of relationship beyond the appearance of the objects. For example, when children separate pots and pans from spoons, forks, and plates, they demonstrate that they are able to distinguish cooking tools from eating tools. Similarly, separating miniature farm animals from zoo animals demonstrates an awareness of each of two subclasses of animals.

Precounting Skills

There are five essential skills that converge when children become interested in quantifying. Each of these skills develops in a variety of ways prior to converging into counting as described in Table 4.2, Growing into Counting. They are the development of

- a sense of set. The ability to recognize a set grows as children make choices about what objects belong together, following the progression described above.

- an awareness of numerical quantity without the use of number. Children show an interest in number when they use the non-numerical quantifying terms such as "more than," "less than," "some," or "a lot." If children are unaware of gross differences in the size of sets, counting is not important to them.

- a familiarity with the sequence of counting words. Reciting the counting words without reference to objects or actions is referred to as *rote counting*.

- a one-to-one correspondence of items between two sets of concrete materials. This skill leads to the ability to match the number words to a set of objects.

- the ability to mentally organize and keep track. This assures that, when children count, they will count each item in a set once, and only once.

There seems to be little evidence that children need to learn these precounting subskills in a particular sequence. However, it is clear that subskills converge in a coordinated action in the form of rational counting when children want to specifically quantify a set of objects or events.

It is important to note that children do not need to read and write numerals using conventional symbols in order to begin rational counting. Reading and writing are not subskills for precounting purposes. The need to record quantitative information in symbolic form emerges as children progress to using counting in order to organize their experiences. When this happens, numerals appear as an important method for representing quantities to which they want to refer later.

Making Curriculum Decisions Using a Map of "Growing into Counting"

Effective use of the curriculum map requires that adults observe children and figure out where they are in their mathematical understandings

Table 4.2
Growing into Counting

Level I: Growing into Counting

Big Ideas: Developmental Indicators	Examples
A sense of set Concrete sets are made up of objects that are viewed as having something in common. The grouping criteria progresses as follows:	
subjective and personalistic (my favorite things)	A toddler using subjective criteria to gather objects of interest and ignore other available ones.
objective properties (same color, shape, size)	A preprimary child sorting leaves by size, or grouping attribute blocks by shape and eliminating shapes that do not fit the groupings.
membership in a class (dogs, vehicles, letters)	A primary age child sorting collections of rocks based on geological categories and eliminating non-rock objects.
Awareness of set as an entity precedes awareness of quantity.	
A sense of numerical quantity One attribute of a set is its quantity without reference to specific number. This is often referred to as the "manyness property of a set" in contrast to other such properties as color, size, or shape.	Use of the quantitative terms such as "more," "more than," "less," "less than," "a lot," "not so many," "some," "a bunch." This emerging sense of quantity is often expressed when distributing food and toys.
Awareness of the manyness property of a set precedes counting.	
Counting words have a consistent sequence. Knowledge of and fluency with the sequence of the set of number words that are used to count without concern for quantifying sets. Familiarity with counting word order (rote counting) precedes counting for a purpose.	The order of counting words is learned in many ways before use in finding out "how many?" Typically, chants and songs involve number recitation.
Items in sets can be matched one-to-one to establish equivalency or nonequivalency. Counting depends upon the child's ability to pair one counting number (from the set of counting numbers) with one object in the set to be counted.	Children create pairs in naturally occurring situations, such as organizing peas on their plate in sets of two, or lining up straws with napkins in preparation for snack.

Table 4.2 (continued)

Level I: Growing into Counting (continued)

Big Ideas: Developmental Indicators	Examples
A sense of numerical quantity (continued) Matching items one-to-one across sets without number precedes counting—matching numbers to the items in a set.	
Counting requires keeping track of the process so that all items are counted only once.	
Accuracy depends on including all items in a set and counting them no more than one time. Although we tend to think of this as a visual task, in fact, understanding the process rests in the mind. The ability to mentally organize while counting is critical to achieving accuracy.	Mental tracking is lacking when children over count by counting objects more than once. Adult organization of sets, such as setting them in a line, only helps if the counter is already beginning to mentally keep track.

Level II: Development of Number Sense

Big Ideas: Developmental Indicators	Examples
Analyzing sets: When sets are grouped and regrouped, the total numerical quantity does not change unless items have been added or removed.	Separating or partitioning sets into smaller groups and recombining to recreate the original quantity.
Understanding of odd and even: When a set is partitioned into two groups by pairing, an uneven set is revealed by an unpaired item.	Dividing sets into subgroups with and without leftover items; e.g., making two equal sets of peas on the lunch plate, sharing and distributing classroom resources.
An empty set is a set with no object or items.	Distributing classroom materials, partitioning sets into one or more groups, constructing with objects, dramatic activities using props

and skills. However, as we watch children proceed through these different levels, it is not always clear how much they understand. Take, for example, the following observation and subsequent conversation:

A mother of a young toddler recently raised the question of how we know when counting takes form for young children. Her son repeatedly uses the number words *one, two, three, four,* and *five* when walking up the stairs to his home. She was initially impressed that her 1½-year-old was counting. But then she wondered whether he was actually counting or imitating what he had heard. She was under the impression that her son was using one number word for each step he took. The question remains, did he have a sense that he was enumerating, that is, counting the actions and tuning into the idea of "how many?" Or was he copying a ritual that he had observed?

In discussion, the mother recalled other observations of her child reciting the number words unconnected to actions. We decided it is likely that he had an intuitive feeling for the relationship between saying a word and climbing a step. He was successfully copying an event he had observed. However, it is not likely at age 1½ years that he was thinking about the number of steps as a set that one describes by counting with numbers. This child had not yet connected the process of counting to the mathematical product of determining "how many steps."

Using the curriculum map in Table 4.2, we can place the child at the point of developing familiarity with the order of the number words and patterning words to action. Our adult role, in this case, is to help children increase their initial familiarity with the counting process and to continue to model the use of the number words. It is worthwhile not only to model the use of number words in action sequences but also in other contexts such as counting food objects or toys. Helping children think about quantity (i.e., "how many") requires that children have increasingly wider exposure to counting for a purpose. Mathematics skills and understanding that initially appear based on an intuitive, or an inner, logic flower into conscious and deliberate use through many experiences fed by peers and adults.

The choice of effective instructional strategies to support emerging counting skills requires identification of the weakest link in a child's developing ability in counting. It is important to note not only the point at which children's accuracy in counting breaks down but also the nature of the error. The three discrete reasons for explaining why the child counter loses accuracy center on the subskills. As we watch, we can see whether

- the child loses track of the sequence of number names in order;
- the child loses continuity in matching one number to one object; or
- the child loses track of the set, counting some objects twice and missing other objects.

How to Help Children Move from Precounting to Counting

The critical piece of information needed to guide the adult in creating opportunities to strengthen children's counting ability is to identify which subskill broke down and at what level. For example, consider a situation in which Pedro is counting fifteen beads that he has just strung: "1, 2, 3, 4, 5, 6, 7, 8, 9, 10, 2-teen, 9, 8, 10, 11." Although he lost track of the sequence of *number words* at number 11 when counting the set of fifteen objects, it was clear by his actions of pointing to each object that he maintained *one-to-one correspondence* between words and objects. This means that he stated fifteen number words as he accounted for each of the fifteen items.

Based on this observation, Pedro needs to have increased opportunities to become familiar with the number word sequences from ten to twenty. While there is little defense for mindless recitation of number words in any educational setting, some legitimate activities can take place in order to help him move toward this goal. The adult can build his familiarity with counting that accompanies high-interest activities by planning activities such as chanting number words that recur in the rhymes of a read-aloud text, singing the number words to accompany rhythm and movement activities, and chanting number words during transitions both in and out of the classroom. Children thoroughly enjoy chants, rhymes, songs, and repetitive refrains. They are prone to repeat the refrains of number words spontaneously during self-directed activities. Once the word sequences are in their language repertoire, they are ready to use number name lists for counting collections and actions.

If, on the other hand, the child has the number words up to fifteen securely memorized, but loses track of the correspondence between the counting words and the objects at the eleventh item, then adults might plan activities that include one-to-one matching between sets such as pairing fifteen circles with fifteen sticks for distribution in advance of a class mural project.

Note that Table 4.2 also lists examples of activities in which children engage as they move along the road map through the critical steps from precounting through beginning computation.

Counting and the Emergence of Number Sense

Number sense refers to the emerging understanding of patterns and relationships when children deal with the numerical quantity of sets.

Children become increasingly aware of several kinds of relationships and consistent patterns as they use number to find out the answer to the question, "How many?" They note that when they count up, as in collecting crayons, the counted set becomes larger. When they distribute a set, as in handing out straws, the original set reduces in number. When they separate or partition and recombine sets, as when organizing raisins before eating, they retain the original quantity.

Children develop the capacity to discover the numerical relationship between a whole set and its parts through counting that occurs during the many experiences with collecting, sorting, grouping, and organizing collections described above. Initially, this increasing fluency takes the form of discovering what happens when they combine (join) sets and when they separate (partition) larger into smaller sets. They progress from ideas of *equal*, identical objects in each set, to *equivalency*, in which there are the same number of objects but not necessarily identical items. Once children incorporate meaningful counting into their repertoires, they use it in an endless variety of ways. For example, daily living activities provoke number use during common events surrounding eating, grocery shopping, taking out and putting away clothing and other household materials, preparing for outings to the park, and social visits. Additionally, number serves children's needs for "fair play" and equal access to materials they use during high-interest, child-directed activities. We often see them using number to distribute materials when they engage in creative drama.

Literature also stimulates spontaneous counting, as children examine pictures of groups of people, animals, and objects. The illustrations prompt them to make connections to text, often through numerical comparisons. A family of pigs with two piglets pictured on one page contrasted with a family of rabbits with four baby rabbits begs comparison; for example, "There are more rabbits. There are only two baby pigs and there are four baby rabbits." The frequent use of number in diverse situations strengthens children's number sense and evolves into computation in a seamless way.

Computation

Although concrete materials initially drive computational thinking, they also provide later support as children meet real-life problems that require computation. Table 4.3 lists the critical points that indicate how children develop their computational skills. The critical points, rather

Table 4.3
Development of Computational Skills

Critical Points	Indicators
Simple computation up to 10 with and without props	Identifying a consistent relationship between the size of the groups that are joined and the size of the group that is created.
Exchange based on equivalency	Trading based upon agreed-upon values, or ratios: *Example*: 2 small beans for one large bean 3 beans for a bean stick 5 red checkers for one blue checker
Sequencing a cluster of sets based on number Interval counting	Place objects or numerals in order beginning with an interval of 1, then 2, then 5, then 10. *Example*: When using pegboard, each successive row has one more peg.
Problem solving: word problems	Figuring out distribution of materials in real-life situations. *Example*: Planning for a cooking activity or a group trip to buy fish.
Computing using written symbols, i.e., numerals; inventing and using rules (algorithms)	Figuring out numerical problems based on written numbers when planning classroom projects. Collecting and interpreting data related to curriculum topics.
Computing: addition and subtraction using double digits, regrouping, and decomposition	Working on word problems related to stories in literature, class projects, and those created by classmates using numbers to 20, 30, 50, 100.

than being tightly sequenced, tend to cluster together as skills and understanding that blend in the progressive development. Some examples appear in the section that follows.

- Simple computation up to ten may also involve responding to real-life problems which take the form of word problems. Typical examples occur when children distribute materials and snacks: "George. You and your partner can each have three pipe cleaners for the project. Please take the amount you will need for both of you."
- Children can make exchanges that are based on equivalency. For example, they can trade ten units of one for one unit of ten when play-

ing games, or the goal might be to earn two blue markers which they can trade for ten white markers.

- Children become fluent with quantitative sequences, as in interval counting by fives.

- Children engage in mental computation and solve word problems. For example, using knowledge of exchange, interval counting, and familiar doubles, children compute word problems without props.

- Children compute by using symbols. This skill emerges as children make connections between the written number and quantities. Since children vary in their development and interest in written number, they may choose to represent actions that combine and partition sets at any point after simple computational thinking begins. It is clear, however, that single-digit computation precedes double-digit computation.

How to Sequence the Level of Difficulty in Word Problems

In the past two decades the work of the Wisconsin University mathematics researchers has made a major contribution to our understanding of the levels of difficulty of word problems and the way children think about solving them (Carpenter et al. 1999). Their work adds important details to the map of content in the area of computation.

We have always known that finding the sum when both addends are given, as in Equation 1, is easier than finding the missing addend when we have only one addend and the sum, as in Equation 2:

Equation 1 $8 + 11 = X$

Equation 2 $8 + X = 19$
$X + 11 = 19$

As a result of this latest research, we now have even more precise information about the level of difficulty related to the location of the missing addend. When the addend is missing from the second position, as 8 plus *blank* equals 19, the child has some clue how to start and therefore the difficulty of this problem is less than when the missing addend is in the first position.

When given a word problem that requires joining two sets, children initially model the problem by representation. First they create each set separately and then join the sets in order to count all the items in the joined set. The materials they use for props may be objects or their fingers.

At the next level, instead of *counting all* the items, they *count on*, beginning with one number in the problem and working toward the other number provided in order to find the missing information. For example, when joining two sets of five and seven, they count on, beginning with either seven or five. The first set is not recounted, but merely serves as the initial place to count on.

Ultimately, they figure out the problem in their heads, using known combinations, such as doubles, or number relationships using combinations of ten.

Other researchers support the finding that children consistently begin with the tens column when computing double-digit numbers in their heads (Kamii & Housman 2000). The implications of these research findings are that children have considerably more ability to think through mathematical relationships than our conventional school mathematics programs give them credit for. In addition, we do children a disservice if we prematurely teach them the addition algorithms. We have a variety of instructional options available to bring mathematics into a broad range of school activities without declaring war on the school choice of mathematics curriculum. What is important is that adults respect children's thinking and use their thinking to uncover more sophisticated ways of figuring out mathematical problems before introducing adult-defined rules for computation.

Concluding Remarks

The maps that define the development of children's number sense can help adults to shape curriculum for the early childhood years. The maps begin with sets and culminate with whole number operations. Young children's development of number concepts and skills intersects with their development of understanding in geometry and measurement that are discussed in the next chapter.

Recommended Reading

Carpenter, T., et al. (1999). *Children's mathematics: Cognitively guided instruction.* Portsmouth, NH: Heinemann. Some of the research findings about children's problem-solving strategies are further illuminated by the CD-ROM accompanying the book.

Curcio, F. R., & Schwartz, S. L. (1997). "What does algebraic thinking look like and sound like with preprimary children?" *Teaching Children Mathematics* 52 (3): 296–300.

Dacey, L. S., & Eston, R. (1999). *Growing mathematical ideas in kindergarten*. Sausalito, CA: Math Solutions.

Fosnot, K., & Dolk, M. (2001). *Young mathematicians at work: Constructing number sense, addition, and subtraction*. Portsmouth, NH: Heinemann. Focus of the research project report is on "learner strategies and the big idea surrounding them." A rich collection of stories from the classroom provides vivid descriptions of the mathematical connections primary children make as they engage in a variety of activities and tasks.

National Council of Teachers of Mathematics (NCTM). (2001). *Navigating through algebra in prekindergarten–grade 2*. Reston, VA: NCTM. Another book in the series described above. It deals with (1) patterns, (2) variables and equality, and (3) relations and functions.

————. (2003). *Navigating through problem solving and reasoning in prekindergarten–kindergarten*. Reston, VA: NCTM. This book is one in a series of guides for developing mathematical understandings and skills. It features a discussion of fundamental ideas followed by suggested activities in the five content strands listed in *Principles and standards for school mathematics* (cited in the References). A CD-ROM accompanies the book as well as "blackline masters."

Whitenack, J., Knipping, N., Loesing, J., Kim, O., & Beetsma, A. (2002). "Supporting first graders' development of number sense." *Teaching Children Mathematics* 9 (1): 26–31. Documents children's acquisition of number sense through a series of activities ranging from initial counting to double digit computation. Describes the activities that revealed the developmental levels as well as the sequence for increasing the complexity of the tasks.

References

Bredekamp, S. (Ed.). (1987). *Developmentally appropriate practice in early childhood programs serving children from birth through age eight*. Washington, DC: National Association for the Education of Young Children.

Carpenter, T., et al. (1999). *Children's mathematics: Cognitively guided instruction*. Portsmouth, NH: Heinemann.

Doverborg, E., & Samuelsson, I. (2000). "To develop young children's conception of numbers." *Early Childhood Development and Care* 162: 81–107.

Greenberg, P. (1984). "Ideas that work with young children: How and why to teach all aspects of preschool and kindergarten math naturally, democratically, and effectively (for teachers who don't believe in academic programs, who do believe in educational excellence, and who find math boring to the max)." Part 2. *Young Children* 49 (2): 12–18, 88.

Kamii, C., & Housman, L. (2000). *Young children reinvent arithmetic: Implications of Piaget's theory*, Chapter 4, pp. 75–65. 2nd ed. New York: Teachers College Press.

Kamii, C., with Joseph, L. (1982). *Number in preschool and kindergarten: Educational implications of Piaget's theory.* Washington, DC: National Association for the Education of Young Children.

———. (1989). *Double column addition.* VHS. New York: Teachers College Press.

Kofsky, E. (1966). "A scalagram study of classificatory development and implications." *Child Development* 37 (1): 191–204.

Monighan-Nourot, P., Scales, B., & Van Hoorn, J., with Almy, M. (2004). *Looking at children's play: A bridge between theory and practice.* New York: Teachers College Press.

National Council of Teachers of Mathematics (NCTM). (2000). *Principles and standards for school mathematics.* Reston, VA: NCTM.

Wann, K., Dorn, M., & Liddle, E. (1962). *Fostering intellectual development in young children.* New York: Teachers College Press.

CHAPTER 5

How Young Children Learn Geometry and Measurement

What a child experiences in the "here and now" depends on that child's previous experiences. Understanding appears in the contrasts of variety; without variation, there is no discernment or learning.— E. Doverborg and I. Samuelsson, "Children's Experience of Shape in Space" (2001)

Two-year-old José was sitting next to his uncle in the back seat as they rode along a country highway. He became excited when he spotted a fire hydrant along the side of the road, declaring "Fi-er. Fi-er." His uncle confirmed that it was a fire hydrant. For the remainder of the ride, every time Jose saw a fire hydrant he chanted "A-na-thur fi-er hi-drant" even though the color of the hydrants changed from red to yellow as they crossed a town line.

José recognized the shape of the fire hydrant and distinguished it from the surrounding environment.

Two second-grade children were working with a geoboard, a flat plastic 7" × 7" object with approximately fifty pegs evenly spaced on the surface. They had just hooked ten rubber bands on the geoboard pegs, in triangular, rectangular, and square shapes. The rubber band shapes overlapped. Now they were collaborating on finding out how many triangles were visible in the mix of lines created by the rubber bands. "Look, there's one in the middle." "Yeah, here's one on this side and another one inside of this square." At first they just searched. After a few minutes, they began taking turns finding the shapes and keeping track by counting.

In these opening vignettes, the children are discovering and using understanding about shapes. The two-year-old was relating to a general shape of an object, a fire hydrant, while disregarding its color. The second-grade children were also narrowing their search to one shape while disregarding the rest of the shapes on the geoboard. The mathematical understanding of the older children emerges in a predictable sequence as children discriminate between shapes in their natural environment.

Just as acquisition of number skills and concepts follow a developmental progression, so, too, does the acquisition of content in geometry and measurement. The progressions serve as the basis for the maps to guide adults as they plan what to teach and how to teach children about geometry and measurement. The maps that follow flow from the list of goals for early childhood learning in geometry and measurement developed by professional mathematics educators.

Several research sources shape current knowledge about how young children develop their geometric and spatial thinking and contribute to the curriculum maps presented in this chapter (Clements 1999; van Hiele 1986). These researchers confirm that children's progress in developing understandings about shape and space conforms to (1) the guidelines for the sequence of learning processes—specifically, that children learn first from concrete experiences and then from increasingly abstract experiences, and they make connections from the known to the unknown along lines of simple-to-complex; and (2) the levels of classification thinking that proceed from matching to sorting, grouping, and classifying. (See Chapter 3 for additional details.)

How Young Children Learn about Geometry

As young children see similarities and differences in both three-dimensional and two-dimensional shapes, they become aware of geometric forms. At first, the global characteristics of three-dimensional objects capture their attention. Later, they increasingly discriminate between standard shapes, such as balls, spheres, cubes, cones, rectangular solids, and cylinders. They become aware of the distinctive shapes on the sides of the three-dimensional objects as well as of two-dimensional shapes, such as circles, rectangles, and triangles. Through the preprimary years, we can see children comparing and contrasting shapes and independently placing like shapes together. Some of the everyday activities that children pursue that contribute to their development of geometric knowledge appear in the following examples:

- The toddler playing with pots and pans collects pots in one group and lids in another.
- The preschooler stacks cans in one pile and the cereal boxes in another.
- The kindergartener collects various sizes of triangles and gives the rectangles to her playmate.
- The primary-grade child sorts pictures of trucks and passenger cars into two groups.

Thus, children make progress in recognizing similarities and differences in shapes, beginning with a group's global characteristics, such as pots and pans, to distinctive attributes, such as trucks contrasted with passenger cars.

How Adults Can Help Children Learn Geometry

The National Council of Teachers of Mathematics recommends, "Instructional programs from prekindergarten through grade 12 should enable all students to . . . analyze characteristics and properties of two- and three-dimensional geometric shapes and develop mathematical arguments about geometric relationships" (NCTM 2000, p. 96). Table 5.1 lists four major standards and what the standards mean for a major segment of early childhood, prekindergarten through grade 2.

Careful study of the NCTM Standards for Pre-K-2 leads to the design of Table 5.2, the first map to guide the curriculum decisions. In Level 1, children observe, compare, and contrast attributes of shapes before they are able to sort shapes. As they collect information by manipulating materials, they begin to connect their actions to the labels that adults provide. After children acquire labels, the materials do not need to be visible when they talk about them. Then, they are able to preplan shape constructions because they are aware of their unique attributes.

Geometry Learning in Action

In the block area, two three-year-old children were working alone in their own space. One child hummed to himself as he aligned blocks, two by two, placing flat sides together. The other child was silently bunching large and

Table 5.1
NCTM Geometry Standard for Grades Pre-K–2

Instructional programs from prekindergarten through grade 12 should enable all students to—	In prekindergarten through grade 2 all students should—
analyze characteristics and properties of two- and three-dimensional geometric shapes and develop mathematical arguments about geometric relationships.	Recognize, name, build, draw, compare, and sort two- and three-dimensional shapes; Describe attributes and parts of two- and three-dimensional shapes; and Investigate and predict the results of putting together and taking apart two- and three-dimensional shapes.
specify locations and describe spatial relationships using coordinate geometry and other representational systems.	Describe, name, and interpret relative positions in space and apply ideas about relative position; Describe, name, and interpret direction and distance in navigating space and apply ideas about direction and distance; and Find and name locations with simple relationships such as "near to" and in coordinate systems such as maps.
apply transformations and use symmetry to analyze mathematical situations.	Recognize and apply slides, flips, and turns; and Recognize and create shapes that have symmetry.
use visualization, spatial reasoning and geometric modeling to solve problems.	Create mental images of geometric shapes using spatial memory and spatial visualization; Recognize and represent shapes from different perspectives; Relate ideas in geometry to ideas in number and measurement; and Recognize geometric shapes and structures in the environment and specify their location.

Source: National Council of Teachers of Mathematics (2000), *Principles and standards for school mathematics* (Reston, VA: NCTM), p. 96.

Table 5.2
Generic Map for Shape Geometry

Recognize two- and three-dimensional shapes by visual means, evidenced when children match and cluster identically shaped objects

1. Sort	2. Label	3. Construct and draw
Cluster and group same-shaped objects of different sizes, different positions or orientations.	Respond to label produced by others. Produce label when shape is visible. Describe attributes and parts of shape when shape is visible.	Discover attributes through constructing and drawing.
Recognize shapes in the environment. Recognize and represent shapes from different perspectives.	Create mental images using spatial memory and spatial visualization. Describe attributes and parts of shape when not in view.	Investigate attributes of shapes. Predict results of constructing and deconstructing.

Relate ideas in geometry to ideas in number and measurement

small cylinders in one group and two different-sized rectangular blocks in another group. Periodically she stopped her actions, looked and smiled.

In the above event the first child was pairing objects based on identical properties of size and shape, while the other child was relating to shape alone irrespective of size. Both of these children are at the initial stages of recognizing shapes.

Meaningful connections between facts and concepts develop as children actively explore relationships in shape geometry and recognize patterns in these relationships.

- Matching shapes occurs in all kinds of situations where children have the opportunity to "play" with materials.
- Finding shapes in the environment occurs both spontaneously and in response to stimulation by others. It requires children to distinguish shapes by mentally framing the selected shape or using a prop to frame observations of parts of objects such as buildings, plants, vehicles.

- Combining shapes to create new shapes occurs with materials that are coordinated. Typical materials are wooden puzzles, collections of attribute blocks, precut paper, and standard cardboard geometric shapes.
- Constructing and altering shapes occurs with materials that children might combine or alter. Typical materials are sticks, pipe cleaners, yarn, cardboard strips, and rubber bands.

Children actively discover the unique attributes of a shape and how it relates to another shape when they construct and deconstruct or take apart shapes in high-interest activities. For example, a triangle retains its critical attributes of being a closed figure with three sides and three angles irrespective of the length of the sides and the degree of the angles. Similarly, children discover that the only attribute that changes when transforming a nonsquared rectangle to a squared rectangle or the reverse is the length of one set of opposite sides.

A Content Map to Teach Two-Dimensional Geometric Shapes

Table 5.3 outlines the developmental sequence of the "big ideas" and how adults might help children make progress in understanding them.

The Language of Shape Geometry. Children label geometric shapes after they have become aware of shape as an attribute of an object, in the same way that they learn to count after they have become interested in the quantity of collections that they make. Contrary to the expectations of many adults, children do not instantly learn to use geometry. This learning occurs over time as children make connections between the adult labels and the objects they use. Repeated exposure to the labels develops familiarity with the terms and equips children to recognize the label. In the beginning, children connect the label used by the adult with the shape when it is in view and then, over time, connect the label with an image they have in their heads. When they begin to use the label in their conversation with peers and adults, it indicates that the label has become part of their functional vocabulary.

Geometry Is More than Shape Labels. Children also need labels for the critical attributes of shapes in order to talk about them and to increase their understanding of the relationship of parts to the whole. Children

Table 5.3
Two-Dimensional Geometric Shapes

Content Map

Plane Geometry Content Sequence of Big Ideas	Children's Learning Strategies and Instructional Implications
2-dimensional shapes vary in terms of open and closed curves, curved and straight edges/sides, and the number of corners and edges/sides	Learn through repeated multisensory examination of collections of objects. Initially distinctive differences in the properties, e.g., in shape and size attract greatest attention. Teach by providing variety of opportunities with different collections and allowing time to examine objects, listening and observing to guide selection of conversation topics, and using shape geometry vocabulary in context: side, angle, corner, curved line, straight line.
2-dimensional shapes can be matched and sorted based on identical attributes of shape and size	Learn by matching shapes, stacking and lining up. Teach by providing collections that invite matching and grouping identical shapes, encouraging comparison and contrast of sorted groups using shape labels as part of the conversation, *using shape labels* in context: triangle, circle, rectangle, squared rectangle.
Objects can have identical shape attributes yet vary in size, orientation, and position —shapes can be grouped based on similar attributes	Learn by sorting or grouping similar plane shapes based on number of sides irrespective of size, constructing and deconstructing standard shapes based on number of sides and angles and length of sides using plastic and graphic art materials and blocks. Teach by providing activities for constructing shapes; using shape vocabulary in context.
2-dimensional shapes can be combined and recombined to create new shapes	Learn by using knowledge of geometric shapes in curriculum activities, inventing of ways to use shapes in expressive art activities. Teach by providing opportunities to use shape knowledge.

learn that triangles have three angles, rectangles have four angles, circles and ovals have no angles, two-dimensional shapes have sides, and three-dimensional shapes have "faces." A teacher's talk with children about their use of shapes during activities helps them to advance their thinking from an intuitive to a conscious level of understanding. Below is a sample list of terms for shape in clusters that include names of labels, descriptors, and attributes.

Shape vocabulary

Name labels	Descriptors	Attributes
circle	circular	no angles, rounded edge
triangle	triangular	3 angles, 3 sides
rectangle	rectangular	4 right angles, 4 sides
squared rectangle	squared	4 right angles, same length/ congruent sides
pentagon	pentagonal	5 sides, 5 angles
hexagon	hexagonal	6 sides, 6 angles
octagon	octagonal	8 sides, 8 angles
rhombus	diamond-shaped	4 angles, opposite sides parallel
curved line	open curve	
cube	cubical	squared faces, 6 surfaces
sphere	spherical	rounded surface
cone	conical	circular base
cylinder	cylindrical	circular ends, rounded sides
rectangular solid	block	rectangular faces, 6 surfaces

Classifying Shapes. Several decades ago when working with kindergarten teachers in Anchorage, Alaska, a couple of visiting mathematics educators alerted me to the dangers inherent in the school practice of prematurely focusing on labels. They asserted that the popular early childhood curriculum activities intended to teach children the difference between a square and a rectangle constitutes inaccurate information. In fact, a square is a rectangle, albeit a special kind of rectangle. The distinguishing characteristics of a rectangle are that (1) it is a quadrilateral—it is a closed figure with four straight-line sides; (2) it is a parallelogram—opposite sides are parallel; and (3) it has four right angles. The definition of a square adds one more attribute to the initial definition of a rectangle: the sides must be equivalent in length. The mathematics educators noted that the long-term problem with leading children to believe that a square is not a rectangle contradicts the big idea that when shapes have a common core of attributes they belong within a class.

Early instruction is very powerful. In my experience, adults who have been taught that squares and rectangles belong to two different classes find it difficult to change that view. Tracking the path that details the position of shapes in a hierarchy of shapes reveals that (1) the square belongs to the class of rectangles, (2) the class of rectangles belongs to the class of parallelograms, (3) the class of parallelograms belongs to the class of quadrilaterals or four-sided figures, and (4) the class of quadrilaterals belong to the class of closed curves or closed figures. This hierarchy is an example of how the core of mathematical learning centers on the need to identify patterns of relationships. The challenge to the adult educator is to keep the door open to permit children to mature in their ability to use classification thinking in shape geometry.

A Content Map to Teach Space Geometry

Space geometry embraces spatial orientation, position, and location.

In preprimary programs, informal curriculum helps young children develop fluency with positional and locational terms. They learn the language of position (next to, over, under) as well as location (on the top shelf) by engaging in, producing, and responding to activities that usually are embedded in music, movement and action games, and clean-up routines. Additionally, over the years early childhood educators have continued to feature the potential spatial learnings associated with block-building and the use of props with construction materials. Recently, educators have integrated spatial awareness in such areas of study as geography (Mitchell 2001). Classroom materials that stimulate construction of models of the physical environment, such as a room arrangement and building with unit blocks, are important resources that help children to develop spatial thinking.

Primary programs that teach spatial geometry tend to place considerable emphasis on paper-and-pencil practice. An undeclared assumption in limiting practice to written exercises is that children have had a rich set of experiences on which to draw. It presupposes that they have both the language and the spatial awareness to translate the world of action to representations on paper. However, written assessment of children's acquisition of knowledge in spatial geometry often reveals an inadequate background of experiences.

The curriculum map that grows out of the rules for sequencing can guide adults to help children develop their spatial understanding. Infants and toddlers first learn to orient themselves in space as they become increasingly mobile and move around, over, under, inside, and outside. Just as shape geometry learning is fed by measurement, so too is spatial understanding. Young children become aware of distance as they explore space, first with their own body and later with objects in the environment.

Young learners integrate the connection between their own location and position. As children investigate space, the adult language describing such investigations helps them extend their learning. The sequence of geometric language use begins when children respond to the language labels that others use, continues when they use language while moving in space, and culminates when they are able to plan how to negotiate in space by using their own mental images. Adults use a variety of terms of position and location to help children extend their understanding of spatial relationships in meaningful contexts:

High, higher, highest	Low, lower, lowest
Inside, outside	
Under, over	
Underneath, on top of	
Below, above	
Before, after	
Forward, backward	
Right, left	
Next to, in between	
Down, up	
Near, nearer	Far, farther

A Content Map to Teach Measurement

The preceding section highlighted the way linear measurement integrates with the geometry of space and location. Young children also have strong interest in attributes of weight, volume, mass, and area as they become increasingly aware of these attributes in their own body and objects in their environment.

Children's initial experiences of measurement begin by making gross comparisons, such as when they compare the weight of a comparatively heavy object with a lighter one by simply lifting them. After they have had repeated experiences with the measurable characteristics of objects, they begin to make initial generalizations that become further refined with additional experiences. The progression follows a similar path for all kinds of measurement. (See also Table 5.4.) When children compare one item to another—for example, the same, heavier or lighter, longer or shorter, more (volume) or less, full or not full, or matching shapes:

1. Children use multiple units of an arbitrary measure to make comparisons, such as unit blocks lined up to measure a double unit

Table 5.4
Overview of the Development of Measurement Concepts

Identical: Matching Amount Using Parallel or Equivalent Amount

To Be Measured	Measuring Tools
A length of wood	Another matching length of wood A strip of cardboard, equal length A strip of paper, equal length
Height of plant	An equal length of cardboard An equal length of pipe cleaner or straw An equal length strip of ribbon
Container of fluid	Identical container, matching height
Weight of a block of wood	Balance scale: find 1 object of equivalent weight.

Arbitrary Measure: Using Convenient Units

To Be Measured	Measuring Tools

The length of a side of a picture	Use as many units as needed:
	    Popsicle sticks
	    Pipe cleaners
	    Straws, toothpicks
	May use different kinds of items or same kind of items to find equivalent lengths, such as 1 pipe cleaner and 1 stick long or 5 toothpicks long.

Container of fluid	Any other container; transfer contents, mark container, and return fluid to original container.
Weight of a block of wood	Balance scale: find several items which weighed together are the equivalent weight of the wood block.

Arbitrary Measure: Using a Given Unit Repeatedly

To Be Measured	Measuring Tools
A length of wood (requires baseline skills)	A toothpick A stick A pipe cleaner
A container of fluid (requires understanding of "full")	A cup A bottle cap
A block of wood	Checkers Plumbers' washers, same size and same material.

block, a bunch of miniature figures used to balance a miniature truck on a balance scale, cubes to cover an interior space in a block structure, pouring juice from a pitcher into identically sized cups.

2. Children make comparisons by repeated use of an arbitrary measure: using one block, rather than a bunch of blocks, over and over again to measure the length of another block.

3. Children make comparisons by use of standard measures: rulers, scales, cups.

4. Children compute measurements: planning for use of materials, beginning with doubles.

This sequence guides the incorporation of measurement in the variety of curriculum activities that depend on it for completion. Measurement needs are pervasive, ranging from projects to conventional academic tasks. They appear in a broad range of activities from cooking and crafts to setting up title pages in writing activities, organizing one's workspace, and maintaining order with classroom materials.

Concluding Remarks

The maps for process–content connections and for mathematical content guide the development of curriculum. The next chapter examines the connection between assessment and teaching.

Recommended Reading

Copley, J. (2000). *The young child and mathematics.* Chapter 6, "Geometry and spatial sense," pp. 105–125, and Chapter 7, "Measurement in the Early Childhood Curriculum," pp. 125–147. Washington, DC: National Association for the Education of Young Children.

Forman, G., & Kuschner, D. (1987). *The child's construction of knowledge: Piaget for teaching children.* Washington, DC: National Association for the Education of Young Children. Provides a rich array of activity suggestions that involve using mathematical thinking and skills in pursuit of discovery and learning.

Gerhardt, L. A. (1973). *Moving and knowing: The young child orients himself in space.* Englewood Cliffs, NJ: Prentice-Hall. Discusses and illustrates spatial learning through movement for young children.

Hardeman, M. (Ed.). (1974). *Children's ways of knowing: Nathan Isaacs on education, psychology and Piaget.* New York: Teachers College Press.

Kamii, C., with Joseph, L. (1982). *Number in preschool and kindergarten: Educational implications of Piaget's theory.* Washington, DC: National Association for the Education of Young Children.

Mitchell, L. (2001). *Young geographers.* New York: Bank Street College of Education.

National Council of Teachers of Mathematics (NCTM). (2001). *Navigating through geometry in prekindergarten–grade 2.* Reston, VA: NCTM. This book belongs to the series described in *Recommended Reading* at the end of Chapter 4. Topics include (1) two- and three-dimensional shapes, (2) location and position, (3) transformations and symmetry, and (4) visualization, spatial reasoning, and modeling. A CD-ROM and list of suggested children's books are included in all books in the series.

———. (2003). *Navigating through measurement in prekindergarten–grade 2.* Reston, VA: NCTM. Chapters deal with (1) comparing and ordering, and (2) using units and tools.

Schwartz, S. L. (1995). "Developing power in linear measurement." *Teaching Children Mathematics* 7: 412–416. Describes a variety of measurement activities that conform with the criteria of "meaningful to young children."

References

Clements, D. (1999). "Geometric and spatial thinking in children." In Copley, J., (Ed.), *Mathematics in the early years,* pp. 119–129. Washington, DC: National Association for the Education of Young Children; Reston, VA: National Council of Teachers of Mathematics.

Doverborg, E., & Samuelsson, I. (2001). "Children's experience of shape in space." *Learning Mathematics* 21 (3): 32–38.

Mitchell, L. S. (2001). *Young geographers.* New York: Bank Street College of Education.

National Council of Teachers of Mathematics (NCTM). (2000). *Principles and standards for school mathematics.* Reston, VA: NCTM.

Van Hiele, P. M. (1986). *Structure and insight: A theory of mathematics education.* Orlando, FL: Academic Press.

CHAPTER 6

The Connection between Assessment and Teaching

The last three chapters provided content maps for the path leading to children's growth in mathematical understanding. This chapter addresses the many decisions related to developing instructional interactions with children. The first part of the chapter deals with the progression from new learning to children's sense of ownership of mathematical understanding and skills. This understanding begins with children's newly acquired learning and continues through the many phases of development that lead to their achievement of understanding or mastery.

Progression from Initial Learning to Mastery

Essentially, the learning process begins with the introduction or discovery of new information or skill. The process continues along a path through repeated and elaborated experiences with the new content or skill. Finally, the new learning leads children toward increased understanding and the acquisition of skills they can use. The teaching role during the introduction of new learning is clearly different from that which occurs when children are testing and expanding their understanding and skills and ultimately making some applications in differing situations. In order to match teaching to the ways in which children learn, adults need to assess what children already know and their level of mastery of the targeted learning. Instructional design decisions reflect an awareness of the kinds of experiences children need to support learning as it progresses from its beginnings to mastery.

Initial Learning

The first stage, involving the beginning experience or contact with unfamiliar information or new skills, occurs when children discover information or a new skill as they pursue interests. It also occurs when a peer or adult shows them something new, such as using two triangles to make a diamond shape or a new way to do something, such as write the number 1.

Repeated Exposure

Repeated exposure to content or skills in identical or similar conditions can help young children move through the first level toward mastery of new learning, whether children have made their own discoveries or have been taught.

Characteristics of this second stage are duplication of the first experiences, followed by expansion into diverse settings and contexts. For example, after discovering that two triangles can be joined to make a diamond, the child might repeat the action a number of times, picking more triangles to create the same effect. Then, multiple experiments with different-sized triangles, and with triangles made of different kinds of materials in diverse settings, moves the learning closer to mastery. At this second stage of acquisition of knowledge, the initial learning is put into a larger context.

Mastery

The third stage reflects mastery. For example, the child purposefully selects and joins triangles for a specific purpose in a craft activity. At this stage, the child understands how to use the knowledge in diverse ways.

Several factors affect the rate of learning toward mastery. The movement from initial mathematical learning toward mastery or ownership of knowledge and skills proceeds along a predictable path *but at an unpredictable rate.* One reason for the unpredictable speed with which a child masters new learning is our lack of knowledge about the child's exposure to this newly introduced content from other sources. Sometimes an adult's assumption that the learning is new is not accurate; it is very difficult for the teaching adults to know whether a child already has been exposed to newly introduced content prior to the initial experiences in the group setting. The child could have been exposed to concepts at home, in the park, or in the grocery store. For example, if a teacher is introducing counting up to five to a group of children, some children may have had many counting experiences elsewhere while others may have had almost no exposure to counting. Adults are often inclined to label a child as a "slow learner" without realizing that the new experience is a first experience for the child, in contrast to other children who have had the experience an unknown number of times in other places. The children who have had no prior experience are not necessarily "slow learners." They are simply *less* experienced with the content.

Developmental differences also account for the varying rates with which children learn school-designated content and skills. Such diverse developmental factors as eye-hand coordination and logical thinking affect the pace of learning in mathematics as well as other areas. This means that we cannot count on precise scheduling of curriculum sequences if we want to assure that children learn mathematics.

Curriculum Design for the Stages of Learning

Adults can teach children to learn at the three levels—discovery, practice, and application.

Design for Discovery

Children continually discover mathematical patterns and relationships. We frequently see them discovering different ways to sort and match sets of materials—all the big trucks and then all the red trucks—or dramatizing home activities—all the dishes in one pile or making sets of one dish and one glass. It is interesting to increase the complexity of experiences by using different materials. For example, children might learn to progress from sorting that is based on how things look, such as grouping all red triangles, to classifying based on the common property that defines class membership, such as all three-sided or three-angled closed-plane figures. Our goal is to facilitate young children's progression from understanding how things look—all the same size dishes—to how they go together—one dish and one glass for eating. The steps they go through as they move toward concepts are

- matching identical objects and engaging in pairing and grouping them;

- matching sets of real objects to pictured sets on cards that allow them to match one object to each picture, such as a red triangular block to a red picture of a triangle, and green circular block to a green picture of a circle;

- matching the quantity of identical pictured sets based on counting without matching one-for-one—in effect, they find two pictures with the same number of red triangles;

- matching the quantity of nonidentical sets based on counting by finding two pictures with the same number of objects, such as five cars and five people; and

- matching numerals to sets, such as finding the numeral that describes the quantity of a set.

Design for Repeated Exposure

Mathematics embedded in high-interest activities helps children test a rule or idea for consistency or strengthen a skill. For example, if children discover that rectangles always have four sides and four corners or angles even though they do not always look the same, a card game using the different types of rectangles along with circles and triangles will engage them in repeatedly using this new idea. (For further reference to formats for games and playful activities, revisit Chapter 2.)

Children may also spontaneously practice using mathematical relationships with materials in everyday events. For example, placing a collection of materials in "size order" occurs when preprimary children line up string beans on their plates by length or when primary children line up their pencils in size order. It also may appear in their craft products, block structures, and drawings.

First-Grade Children Link Literature and Geometry for the Stages of Learning

Application

An example of one teacher helping first-grade children integrate their study of geometry and literature provided an opportunity for children to apply what they have learned.

The following sequence of integrated curriculum activities occurred over a period of days and weeks. These activities began with a Chinese folktale in a segment of a literacy unit that included folktales in which characters change shape.[1]

Grandfather Tang's Story (Tompert 1990) is a Chinese folklore tale in which the characters transform from one animal into another by repositioning one or several of the seven geometric shapes known as tangrams. (See Figure 6.1.)

After listening to the teacher read the book, the first-grade children discussed the plot, the characters, and the illustrations. They made connections between the story line in this folktale and *The Raven* (McDermott

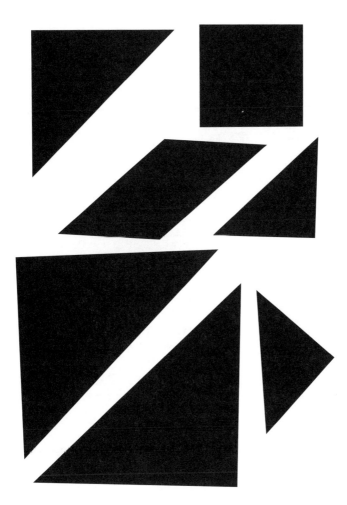

Figure 6.1. Tangrams

1993), another folktale they had just studied in which the main character transforms from one shape to another. After the discussion, the children partnered to reread it and to examine ways in which the *tans* were repositioned to transform the shapes to create new characters. They discussed animals they would like to create with the tangrams.

After further discussion about the changes in the characters, the adult gave each child a seven-piece tangram set that included two identical large triangles, one medium-sized triangle, two identical small triangles, one square, and one parallelogram (Figure 6.1). The adult encouraged the children to manipulate the *tans* and find out how they combine and recombine to create new shapes. As the children discovered patterns of relationship, the teacher helped clarify the vocabulary that described the children's shape reformations:

- Two large triangles with the longest sides adjoining become a square, and a similar square figure is constructed with two small triangles.
- Two triangles placed with short sides facing create a larger triangle.
- Two triangles can completely cover the parallelogram.
- Two small triangles and the parallelogram completely cover the large triangle.
- Two small triangles at opposite sides of a square create a parallelogram.

After manipulating the tans for a sufficient period to exhaust the initial discoveries, the children were invited to compose their own short story of an animal that transforms into another animal by changing shape. As they busily engaged in creating and then changing their own figures by moving the tangram pieces, their comments reflected the full range of learning levels identified earlier—discovery/initial learning, practice through repeated actions, and application of understandings to complete a task:

- Discovery: "Hey look! When I moved this triangle from the front to the back, it's a tail for the dog."
- Practice through repeated actions: "Look. I can do it this way, the triangle and the triangle. But if I put the square here, it's still a rabbit, but different. And then I can make two triangles again."
- Application: "I know what I'm gonna do. I'm gonna make a house with a roof and a door. See! The two triangles make my roof . . . and. . . ."

When the children finished composing and illustrating their stories, they wrote their own text and shared it with classmates. "I changed my rabbit to a wolf. I moved the triangle from the head to the tail." It was interesting to note that the children's illustrations captured the unique characteristics of the animals they represented as modeled in the folktale—large ears for a rabbit and a big tail for a squirrel.

In this activity, literacy integrated with mathematics and science. Each subject area was critical to the learning outcomes. The teaching role included introducing new learning (the literature book and tangrams), clarifying learning in process, and extending learning by creating application tasks. The sequence of learning opportunities conformed with process sequences, moving from concrete to abstract and known to unknown. The content allowed for a range of knowledge in (1) literacy learning—reading, writing, listening, and speaking, (2) life science—characteristics of animals, and (3) mathematical properties of geometric forms.

The Role of the Teacher

Teachers decide how to design instruction by considering children's level of achievement—new learning, practice, or application. In professional development conversations with teachers over the past decade, the ideas of *leading, feeding,* and *seeding* have emerged as ways to think about and discuss curriculum decisions.

The teachers agreed that the instructional design ideas *seeding, feeding,* and *leading* helped them to select teaching strategies.[2]

- The role of *leading* is the most familiar, the one in which the teacher transmits information through a wide range of oral, written, and modeling strategies. This role serves the function of introducing new information and demonstrating new skills. It also can serve to guide practice.

- The role of *feeding* takes the form of supporting acquisition of information by offering language, fostering development of understanding by raising questions about an ongoing event, and strengthening skills by validating the relationship between actions and outcomes.

- The role of *seeding*, in contrast to the other two roles, is one of "putting learning in their way" by setting out resources and then observing what happens.

Adults view the leading role as most closely associated with initial learning. Adult-directed activities introduce new content across the span of several events, so that the children are more likely to retain and use it. For example, in the preprimary program, after introducing measuring tools such as balance scales, the placement of these scales in an activity center with other materials moves the direct teaching role from *leading* to *seeding*. If children respond to the *seeding* effort by using the tool to compare weight measures of some of the objects, opportunities arise for the teacher to *feed* the developing awareness and understanding of balance and congruency in weight by posing problems that children can solve at an interest center. For example, if children discover that five poker chips balance the scale when there is one kindergarten unit block on the other side, the discovery can be fed by wondering how many poker chips they would need to balance two unit blocks on the scale.

Feeding helps a child extend her/his understanding about a relationship. In the following vignette, the adult role helped the child uncover and clarify his understanding about incremental quantities. The following exchange occurred between Eli and his teacher on a kindergarten school trip.

> Eli (after reading a numbered street sign): "What is two-three?"
>
> T: "What do you mean? Do you want me to tell you what the number two-three is, or do you want to know how much is two and three more?"
>
> Eli (pauses): "How much is two and three?"
>
> The teacher held up two fingers on one hand and three on the other, inviting him to count.
>
> Eli counted five. (At the next corner): "What is two and four?"
>
> T: "Do you want to know what number is two-four or how much is two and four more?"
>
> Eli: "How much is two and four?"
>
> The teacher held up two fingers on one hand and four on the other.
>
> Eli counted to six. (At the next corner): "How much is two and five?"
>
> T: Two and three is five. Two and four is six. How much do you think two and five is?"
>
> Eli (pauses): "Seven."
>
> T: "How did you figure that out?"
>
> Eli: "Three-five, four-six, five-seven."

In this vignette, the teacher successfully followed the child's interest as she began to *feed* his understanding of the increment of two numbers as he moved from an intuitive to a conscious level of understanding.

"Teachable moments" offer prime opportunities for *feeding*. Teachable

0	1	2	3	4	5	6	7	8	9

Figure 6.2.

moments occur when children are in the midst of discovering, experimenting, and solving problems in activities of their own choosing. The power of the teachable moment is that it capitalizes on children's interests, setting the stage for us to model meaningful ways for them to use mathematics as a tool to improve their quality of life. The adult involvement can be (1) a momentary contribution, such as adding information or providing language labels; (2) validating strategies a child is using; or (3) an interaction that elicits children's thinking or reactions, helping them to clarify a problem to be solved or one that has just been solved. The following vignette illustrates a momentary contribution.

> Two children were engaged in an activity that required counting, matching numerals to a set of numbers and ordering the sets, zero–nine, on a cardboard strip with spaces marked (see Figure 6.2). One of the children had placed a 7 card on the strip. When she drew a 9, she looked at her strip, and then placed the card on the last box. When I asked her how she figured it out, she shrugged. I restated the question. "How did you know where to put the 9 card?" She answered, "I don't know." Next, I changed the thrust of the question to feed her thinking. "Did you count up from the 7 to 9 or did you just know that the 9 is the last number on the line?" She responded, "I just knew nine was here" as she pointed to the end of the strip.

Until I provided the language and the options, the child was unable to articulate that she knew where the nine belonged because of its location rather than as part of the sequence of numbers. In contrast, the other child at the table did not need this "feeding" role.

> After accurately placing a 5 card with the accompanying numeral on the strip, he drew a card that represented 7. He counted the items in the picture, retrieved the numeral 7 and placed both in the appropriate box without appearing to count. When I asked him, "How did you figure out where to place that card?" he responded by pointing to the 5 card and saying, "six, seven" and "that's how I know."

Teachable moments occur during so many different kinds of activities that adults need to make choices and be careful not to intrude on children's independent efforts to construct understandings about mathematical patterns and relationships.

A Comparison of Two Models: Teaching Mathematics Actively or Incidentally

Early childhood researchers in Sweden have reported on the powerful possibilities that flow from coordinating the three instructional strategies of *leading, feeding,* and *seeding* when combined with both content and process sequences (Doverborg & Samuelsson 2000). Two teachers who were both using programs with primary emphasis on action-based activities chose different approaches to incorporating mathematics into the integrated curriculum. One designed an active teaching approach to mathematics, while the other chose an incidental teaching approach.

Active Teaching Approach

The mathematical focus on shape in space was framed in a thematic study of structures. The activities in this model followed the sequencing guidelines discussed in Chapter 3, specifically, moving in stages from concrete to abstract, from the familiar or known to unknown, and from simple to complex.

- The teachers began by *leading* a set of activities featuring shape in space. They shared a postcard they received from one of the children that pictured an odd-shaped house. A discussion about shapes evolved, setting the context for children to engage in a variety of activities that included constructing and drawing houses and discussing the shapes that were showing up.

- Teachers shifted to *feeding* by clarifying and extending children's thinking through discussion as they worked on their own projects.

- They *seeded* the activity by silently placing additional kinds of supplies in the supply boxes when they noticed a need.

- Successive teacher-initiated activities fulfilling the *leading* role included (1) taking a walk through the neighborhood looking at such structural features as balconies, porches, doors, windows, and such associated features as fences and gates; (2) designing and constructing different structures with precut shapes and three-dimensional materials; (3) making models of environmental features, such as fences; and (4) making puzzles by cutting pictures of houses into parts.

- Opportunities to increase awareness of shape in space led to further *feeding*. The teachers encouraged children to (1) compare and contrast structural shapes and spaces and to take different perspectives from different vantage points, (2) talk about what they were doing, (3) decide what they planned to do next; and (4) reflect together on expected and unexpected outcomes.

In this approach, the teachers featured situations where children could think about and reflect on the geometry content in their activities.

Incidental Teaching Approach

In the incidental teaching approach, integrated curriculum activities in the form of themes shaped the program. The study of shape in space as well as other mathematical topics occurred incidentally within a theme as children expressed awareness of details about shape in space. In addition, the teachers engaged children in non-theme-related mathematical tasks, such as looking at different shapes in their surroundings, making collections, and using shapes in games.

The Power of a Unified Instructional Design

The most interesting finding by these researchers was that for children in the experimental class, there was a notable advantage in children's ability to represent three-dimensional figures at the end of the year and again sixteen months later. The researchers concluded that the focused sequence of activities, one in which the teachers had developed a content map as a guide, "helped children create a relationship between concrete everyday life and more abstract thinking, which is necessary for further theory building" (Doverborg & Samuelsson 2000, p. 38).

In this model, *leading*, following a general content path, takes the primary role to activate learning, while *feeding* and *seeding* take the primary role in supporting children's increasing understanding of mathematical patterns and relationships.

These same researchers have reflected in another study on children's development of number concepts that "content develops in interaction with children" (Doverborg & Samuelsson 2000, p. 104). Success depends upon the match between the children's ability to deal with the content and the way in which teachers interact with them to help make the content accessible. The *feeding* role described above is probably the most challenging, because it requires connecting with children's thinking as part of the interaction. If an adult misreads a child's focus and understanding, the moment disappears and may or may not come again. On the other hand, if teachers err in connecting to the child's understanding while *leading*, then the opportunity to return to the content in a different way is always available. Therefore, assessment considerations play an integral role in instructional decisions about when and how to engage in *leading, feeding,* and *seeding* learning.

How to Assess What Young Children Understand

In order to develop an instructional design, common sense as well as professional know-how dictates that we need to have an understanding of what the children know and can do in a variety of situations. Two of the benchmarks that define major shifts in assessment practice during the past two decades are those of moving away (1) from "assessing specific facts and isolated skills" to "assessing students' full mathematical power," and (2) from a single assessment tool while moving toward offering "multiple opportunities to demonstrate their full mathematical power" (National Council of Teachers of Mathematics 1995).

The most direct sources of information about a child's mathematical learning are two-fold: (1) through testing, using nationally standardized and/or locally generated tests, and (2) through information collected in the living context of the classroom, by observing, interacting with children, and analyzing children's work samples (Wortham 2005). In addition, we can tap information reported by adults who know the child, such as relatives at home and other persons in the community, although the helpfulness of this information depends upon the degree to which the assessment criteria of other people conform with our own.

The field of testing has taught us the importance of obtaining reliable and valid information on both developmental and educational progress. However, this wisdom poses some serious challenges in early childhood settings. Young children's initial mastery of learning, whether from self-propelled activities or direct instruction, tends to be unstable; young children may demonstrate new learnings one day and fail to demonstrate them the next. Similarly, they may demonstrate the learning only when we test for it in the exact same form and situation in which they learned it and not use it in similar situations. Professional educators' organizations are currently engaged in dialogue about assessment and testing in early childhood because they question what constitute valid and reliable measures of children's learning (NCTM & NAEYC 2002).

The Issue of Resistance to Standardized Testing

Effective education prepares learners to communicate what they know and to do so in both formal and informal assessments. In addition, enduring educational goals include the need for children to acquire stable critical skills and understanding that they can use effectively at relevant times and places.

Children need to be able to demonstrate their skills and understanding in a variety of contexts. Assessment, in a true sense, embraces a wide range of tools and taps a variety of conditions for eliciting a child's knowledge, skills, and understanding. Standardized tests, together with observations and work samples, can provide information about what children know and can do.

If skills are securely in children's repertoires, they can use them under most conditions. In the final analysis, standardized tests are an integral part of an industrialized and technological society and serve the needs of such a society by assuring that those hired to fulfill responsibilities have the skills and understanding needed. Simultaneously, nonstandardized observations of and conversations with children in a variety of contexts and the study of children's work samples provide assessment information about young children's understanding and skills for teachers to use in planning ongoing activities.

It is our deep commitment in early childhood education that the responsibility of schooling is to equip students to function effectively in the many phases of life in which they participate. One of these phases involves immediate tasks, for which they need to select and use the mathematical skills that serve the purpose. Another phase requires them to demonstrate what they know. However, experience has taught us that assessment of young children's mathematical skills and understanding is considerably more effective and valid in the natural events of their daily lives than in formal test settings. Acquisition of reliable and valid information requires a well-educated eye and skill in shaping assessments that can be embedded in comfortable settings for the children.

Other Sources of Assessment Information

On a daily basis, the primary source of information about children's mathematical skill and understanding comes from observing how they use and talk about mathematical relationships during routines and high-interest activities. Additional information is available from analysis of work samples collected over a period of time (Wortham 2005). The younger the child, the more we depend upon repeated observations as a measure of what they know and can do. The greatest challenge we face in relying on nonstandard assessments is to establish reasonable and useful systems for collecting, organizing, and analyzing observation information. *Reasonable* refers to the time needed to collect and analyze information; *useful* refers to mutual agreement upon what skills and understandings are critical and what evidence reflects these important learnings.

Agreement on what constitutes the essential elements of mathematics knowledge and skills during the early childhood period, birth to eight years, is difficult. To successfully assess the level of a child's mathematical ability in order to design curriculum and instructional activities, we need not only to understand the mathematical content but also to agree upon criteria to analyze progress. The content maps discussed in Chapters 4 and 5 address this challenge.

Collecting and Sorting Assessment Information

The most reliable ways to find out what knowledge and skills children possess is to (1) watch them in action, (2) listen to their talk when they are pursuing their own interests and interacting with their peers, (3) engage in authentic conversation about their work, and (4) collect work samples. Collecting observational data using a simple recording form can provide a wealth of readily accessible information about children's active use of mathematical ideas. The format suggested in Table 6.1 can serve to assess an individual child or group of children periodically for several weeks. Adults can record how children use mathematical skills and understanding during adult-led activities such as music, movement, and games, and in naturally occurring events during the course of the day. For example, snacks and crafts stimulate rich conversations about quantity, size, and shape. Games, music, and movement activities can reveal children's spatial sense, along with their use of number.

In addition to recording children's use of mathematical skills and un-

Table 6.1
Record of Spontaneous Use of Mathematical Skills and Investigation of Mathematical Relationships in Natural Contexts and High Interest Activities

Date _____ Context (activity in progress) _____

Children's Names	Observed Children's Actions	Children's talk	Mathematical Skills/ Understandings Reflected
Example: Susan and Johanna	After two double graham crackers were distributed, Susan broke both in half. Johanna pushed both Susan's halves together and lined up her unbroken ones alongside.	Susan declared, "I have more than you." Johanna answered, "Oh no! Look, they are the same."	Numerical quantity overrides logic of amount. Can reverse action, and conserve quantity up to 4 items.

derstanding in naturally occurring events, the same format can record information during teacher-directed activities that elicit children's thinking and their independent follow-up. Periodic profiles of children offer necessary information to plan for *leading* and *feeding* individual as well as small group activities.

Table 6.2 illustrates a format for collecting and recording information about young children's knowledge of and skills about number and computation. The adult will need to select the skills that reflect the general expectations for a specific age group. For example, if most of the children are progressing from reciting numbers at an interval of two to using interval counting to understand quantities, the teacher can plan movement activities that focus on "moving forward with every other number"—(one stand), two, jump, (three stand), four jump—or a board game can feature jumping by twos along the path. These activities support the goal of using interval counting purposefully and with understanding.

Observing, Analyzing, and Responding to Mathematical Errors

The major difference between knowing and not knowing is exposed when we make a mistake. Errors mark the starting point for the next

Table 6.2
Class Profile: Number and Computation

Skill	Skill Level	Predominant Pattern	Most Popular/Most Frequently Observed Contexts	
	Range	Typical/Average Level	Teacher-Directed Activity	Spontaneous: Naturally Occurring Activities
Counting				
Rote counting without reference to objects in a set				
Rational counting: using number to find out "how many?"				
Interval counting: rote				
Interval counting referring to actions or objects				
Ordinal Number				
Rote: reciting without reference to objects				
Meaningful: locating and positioning objects in ordinal sequence				

learning task (Kamii & Housman 2000). If we already knew how to achieve a particular goal or solve a specific problem, there would be no mistake. It is only when things do not turn out as we expect that we realize there was something that we did not know. Mistakes occur when the activity requires understanding or skills we have not yet learned. They also occur when our knowledge or skills are not well-enough learned to be useful, usually because they were only partially learned or not used often enough to be incorporated into the permanent repertoire of knowing.

Teachers can use observed mistakes to understand instructional needs. Knowing what children need and finding ways to engage them in learning are separate teaching decisions that depend upon one another. If the activity matches the need but fails to capture interest, the child is not likely to engage in it long enough to serve the purpose. If the task is too complex, even though it captures interest the child will be frustrated trying to complete an activity without the necessary skills.

Table 6.3 illustrates follow-up possibilities for meeting mathematical learning needs that are revealed in mistakes.

It is not always easy to peg the nature of the learning that is occurring by just observing. Take, for example, this recent observation. The task in which the child was engaged focused on locating numbers in the sequence from 0 to 19. The worksheet that accompanied the activity was a five-by-four grid with the numerals 0–19 in order (see Figure 6.3). The cue card listed 3 and 5, directing the user to find the number in between. The child touched 3 and 4, and then touched 3 again. After a few seconds, he circled the numeral 2.

Without the benefit of interviewing the child, we can only make an initial analysis of his thinking. It looks as if he was confusing the locational term "in between" (geometry) with the serial order relationship in the number sequence. Since no number appeared on the line after four that would allow him to *surround* the 4, he reverted to the *next to* location. In terms of the guidelines for sequencing discussed in the previous chapter, the simple to complex rule would indicate he needs more experience with the sequence of numbers without the distraction of a grid format and finding the next item on a grid that is based on an ordered set with which he is familiar, such as picture cards of a familiar story.

Concluding Remarks

Instructional design is directly related to where children are along the path from initial learning to mastery. Instructional strategies for introducing new learning or supporting acquisition to mastery include *leading*, as in direct instruction, *feeding* during teachable moments, and *extending*, when children are involved in using what they know to solve problems involving mathematical patterns and relationships. Sources for assessing this information include observation as well as work sample.

The mathematics curriculum takes shape not only in the context of the instructional design but also in the ways that adults communicate and in-

Table 6.3
Analyzing and Responding to Children's Mathematical Errors or Misunderstandings

Children's Talk and Actions	Mathematics Error or Misunderstanding	Suggested Immediate Response	Suggested Follow-up Activities
(Taken from observation in Table 6.1 with a different scenario) After two double graham crackers were distributed, Susan broke both her crackers in half and declared to Johanna, "I have more than you." Johanna complained to the teacher that Susan had more graham crackers than she did.	Confusing number of items with size of items.	I wonder how it would look if Susan put her two half crackers together next to your one whole cracker.	Stimulate dividing and recombining materials. Example: When using play dough, break up a ball into 2 parts, then recombine; break into 3 parts, then recombine. Talk about always having the same size ball when recombined.
Andrew was counting the animals in the illustration of the story the adult was reading: "1, 2, 3, 4, 5, 7, 8, 6, 7, 8," pointing to one animal with each number recited.	Unstable mastery of the counting numbers above 5, but stable mastery of one-to-one matching of a number name to an animal.	Count together with him without hesitation and verify the final number.	Variety of experiences counting sets up to 10, matching another set to verify accuracy. Example: counting 8 napkins to distribute to children at table.
A child was figuring out how many stars she needed to decorate the 4 hats she had drawn on her book cover. She wanted 4 stars for each hat. She took a handful of stars and started counting. When she had gathered 9 stars, she stopped and looked at her drawing and then kept on counting up to 13. Then she began pasting and finally complained that she didn't have enough.	Does not have a strategy for creating equal sets or computing 4×4.	Ask the child to clarify the plan and then together check to see how many hats have the desired number. Finally count the spaces that have not been filled.	Provide a variety of opportunities to figure out "how many" are needed to create several equivalent groups. Example: distributing snack, planning seating arrangements for a trip.

0	1	2	3	4
5	6	7	8	9
10	11	12	13	14
15	16	17	18	19

Figure 6.3.

teract with children. The next chapter further explores authentic dis-course, instructional questions, and hidden messages in "teacher-talk."

Notes

1. From W. Shilling & S. Schwartz (1996), "Changes," curriculum unit written for the CUNY Literacy Enhancement Project, City University of New York, 1996.

2. I am grateful for the help given in framing these ideas over a period of two years by the professional teaching staff in New York City Community School District 27 Queens, under the leadership of the Director of Early Childhood, Dr. Sherry Copelend.

Recommended Reading

Ginsberg, H., Inoue, N., & Seo, K. (1999). "Young children doing mathematics." In Copley, J. (Ed.), *Mathematics in the early years*, pp. 88–101. Reston, VA: National Council of Teachers of Mathematics; Washington, DC: National Association for the Education of Young Children. The unique contribution of these authors is the "coding system for the analysis of explicit mathematic activities" in the appendix of the chapter. The system looks at children's mathematical behavior in four areas: (1) mathematics content observed, (2) contexts of the actions, (3) the social interaction accompanying the action, and (4) the types of play activities observed.

Martin, D. (2002). *Elementary science methods: A constructivist approach*. 3rd ed. Belmont, CA: Wadsworth/Thomson Learning. Although this book is primarily concerned with science education, Chapter 7 provides some of the best design formats, assessment techniques, and rubrics for authentic assessment of children's information processing skills and attitudes as learners. At the end of the chapter the author lists "assessment techniques customized to learning styles."

Whitin, D., & Wilde, S. (1992). *Read any good math lately? Children's books for math-*

ematics learning K–6. Portsmouth, NH: Heinemann. Discusses a variety of ways to use children's books as a steppingstone to exploring mathematical problems and uncovering patterns and relationships.

References

Doverborg, E., & Samuelsson, I. (2000). "To develop young children's conception of numbers." *Early Childhood Development and Care* 162: 81–107.
———. (2001). "Children's experience of shape in space." *For the Learning of Mathematics* 21 (3): 32–38.
Kamii, C., & Housman, L. (2000). *Young children reinvent arithmetic: Implications of Piaget's theory*. 2nd ed. New York: Teachers College Press.
McDermott, G. (1993). *The raven*. New York: Harcourt, Brace.
National Council of Teachers of Mathematics (NCTM). (1995). *Assessment standards for school mathematics*. Reston, VA: NCTM. National Council of Teachers of Mathematics (NCTM) & National Association for the Education of Young Children (NAEYC). (2002). *Early childhood mathematics: Promoting good beginnings*. Washington, DC: NAEYC; Reston, VA: NCTM.
Tompert, A. (1990). *Grandfather Tang's story*. New York: Crown.
Wortham, S. C. (2005). *Assessment in early childhood education*. 4th ed. Upper Saddle River, NJ: Pearson, Merrill, Prentice Hall.

CHAPTER 7

How Adults Can Communicate with Young Children about Mathematics

"How did you know to bring me eight spoons for these children?"
"I just looked and I saw."
"What did you see?"
"I saw two tables."

"When you picked this strip of paper to paste on your placemat, how did you know it was going to fit here?"
"I don't know. I just did."

"How come you sorted the trucks into two groups?
"Just 'cause!"

When asked by adults to explain their mathematical thinking, young children often respond with simplistic statements that grossly understate the complexity of their intuitive understandings. Even less revealing are responses that are shrugs: "I don't know," or "I just knew." While early mathematical learning begins with children's use of physical materials, their thinking far outstrips their ability to talk about the knowledge they are generating during these events. In order to create a setting for conversation, adults need to help children transform their thoughts into oral language. This requires serious examination of how we talk to children.

In essence, the way adults communicate alerts children to the expectations for teaching and learning interactions. There is a distinct difference between the modes of talking that inform children or test them and those which seek to engage children in the discussion of ideas and the expansion of their thinking.

On the one hand, the culture of teaching has a long history of information transmission with minimal time devoted to thoughtful discussions. Traditionally, teaching in the form of direct instruction takes place in large groups: "Today we are going to learn about. . . ." In this context, the adult uses the questioning strategy to find out how much the children have learned about content that the teacher presented: "Let's review. Who can tell me . . . ?" In order to respond, children need to recall rapidly rather than take time to think about how the new information fits with what they already know.

On the other hand, research on teachers' use of questions has revealed that their efforts to shift from the use of questions that provoke thinking rather than recall also require a change in timing and pacing. Researchers found that teachers typically allow only two to three seconds for children to answer, clearly not enough time to "think" (Rowe 1986). Thinking about patterns and relationships requires more time than remembering facts.

Although most of us experienced vibrant conversations with teachers during the schooling years, such events rarely occurred during the early childhood years. It is my premise that mind-stimulating discussions depend upon authentic conversations, ones in which there is genuine interaction. Authentic discussion is integral to the task of empowering young children to be independent thinkers.

Establishing the Climate for Authentic Interactions

In the exchange of talk during conversations, *authentic* implies that each person in the interaction is participating honestly. This can only occur if the participants feel safe in testing out ideas with those present. In a risk-safe setting, the following attributes of authentic discourse emerge:

- The questioner is seeking information that he or she does not possess. This eliminates the usual "lesson entry" in which the teacher questions children in order to find out if they retained what was taught yesterday. If, in fact, yesterday's information is needed to pursue the conversation, then the class reviews the content together in order to proceed with today's activity without "testing" children. For example, after a prior sorting and re-sorting activity using three-, four-, and five-sided shapes in various colors, the teacher might begin a review with, "Remember the other day when we were looking at different geometric shapes and grouping them? Today we are going to figure out how to change a shape, so think about those shapes you had last time and let's share what you did with them." In this example, children are invited to recall without the implication that one person will be right and others will be wrong. The adult uses the questioning format to focus children on recalling their own experience. The strategy is authentic because the asker does not know what each child recalls.

- The information-giver assumes that the persons to whom he or she is giving information do not possess the information. In the above example, the focus on personal recall assures that responder that the questioner does not know the information.
- Collaborative review of shared experience takes place so that each participant can contribute to the review. Once participants share personal recall, they can pool information for all members to use.
- Participants are active in the process of joint planning or problem-solving; that is, plans and problem's solutions are not set in advance. The new task is framed so that children have the opportunity to pursue their own ideas, such as "Pick one of the shapes and think about how you might change it." The sharing adds to the thinking of all the members of the group.

The National Council of Teachers of Mathematics and mathematical researchers who explore how children think have spurred increased emphasis on the importance of discourse (Carpenter et al. 1999; Fosnot & Dolk 2001; Kamii & Housman 2000; NCTM 1989). Their work reveals the power of using discourse in mathematics to foster children's ability to understand patterns and relationships. In the process of sharing ideas, children increase the clarity of their own thinking, as well as have the opportunity to be exposed to other points of view.

It is important to note, however, that the entire mathematics curriculum is not necessarily implemented through discourse. Initial learning frequently takes place through modeling and explanation as well as guided discovery. Practice occurs in a variety of contexts that include games and playful repetition, as discussed in Chapter 2. Periods of genuine discussion, or *authentic discourse,* have very different attributes than periods devoted to transmission of information. Time to think is an essential element to build into any plans for discourse.

Authentic Conversations with Young Children: A Unique Challenge

Major synonyms for "authentic" are "genuine," "trustworthy," "in good faith," and "with sincerity of intention." In essence this means the questioner is seeking information.[1] Moreover, in the course of conversation, information is exchanged and each participant has an opportunity to contribute to the content of the conversation. In order to initiate and extend authentic conversations, it is necessary to tune in to the context and nature of the emerging mathematical understandings reflected in young children's actions and interactions (Schwartz & Brown 1995). As noted in earlier chapters, a major portion of young children's understanding of mathematical ideas grows out of their experiences in action-based learning environments. They build their mathematical understanding using concrete materials as tools with which to think. Through manipulation of materials, they

- discover patterns and relationships,
- test their mathematical understandings and practice use of skills through many repetitions, and
- apply their understandings of mathematical relationships to build models of their ideas and to solve problems in daily living.

In their activities they share their thoughts with peers and adults at regular intervals. Observation of children's actions and conversations reveals how they are discovering mathematical patterns and relationships. With preprimary children, initial manipulation of such materials as pegboards, blocks, paints, puzzles, miniature cars, and balls feeds the process of finding out about patterned relationships in the many areas of mathematics—number, space and location, symmetry, shape and size, distance, weight, and volume.

At the water table, three prekindergarten children, using sifters and funnels, began comparing the speed with which the water moved through the funnel.
"Look, my water is running faster."
"Oh no! Mine is."
"No, look at mine. It's really fast."

With primary-grade children, discovery of relationships occurs in both naturally occurring and planned curriculum activities throughout the day. In planned curriculum activities, children make discoveries when teachers provide enough time to explore possibilities, such as when working with geometric shapes or experimenting with the path and speed of pendulums.

> The children were asked to make a rectangle using shapes from a set of standard shapes.
>
> "Look. I got it. See two triangles."
>
> "Yeah but mine is different . . . two squares. And I can do it with four squares, too. Look."
>
> "Hey. The two squares together aren't squares any more."

Observation also reveals how children are testing their emerging mathematical understandings. With preprimary children, repetition that often seems endless to us helps children to confirm or negate emerging understandings. On the pegboard, the repeated sequence of red–blue looks the same no matter how many pegs are lined up. When rolling cars, the harder you push the car the further it travels—every time. With primary-grade children, repetitive use of concrete objects to solve similar mathematical problems leads to confirmation of emerging understanding of mathematical patterns and relationships. The use of concrete materials as props for computation precedes skill in mental and written computation. Similarly, repeated use of props in geometry precedes mental imagery of how shapes combine to form new shapes.

In essence, communication follows initial discovery rather than preceding it. First, young children begin constructing mathematical understanding as they use materials. Their first form of communication tends to be with body language, pointing and gesturing. As they acquire oral language the opportunity to talk about what they are doing serves to move intuitive knowledge to the conscious level. Interactions with others lead to the exchange of perceptions, thereby opening up a new vista of possibilities. Communication serves to extend their mathematical ideas and understanding as they increasingly organize their understandings for retrieval, use, and development (Katz & Chard 2000).

Instructional Strategies to Connect Conversation with Actions

The major thrust of the early childhood mathematics education literature today rings with the messages, "catch them thinking mathematics" and "catch them doing mathematics." (Curcio, Schwartz, & Brown 1996; Dacey & Easton 1999; Greenberg 1993). However, "students can be on task with manipulatives and not with mathematics" (Capps & Pickreign 1993). An essential instructional strategy when we observe mathematical thinking in action is to introduce conversation focusing on the mathematics that is connected with their actions. A critical question at this point is, "How do we enter the child's thinking world and make a contribution without overriding their thinking with our adult interpretations?" The teaching strategies we have at our command are to validate, review, and extend or challenge. Each of these strategies can meet the standard of authenticity while meeting communication goals for mathematics in a particular way.

Validating supports the child's growing sense of mathematical relationships. By agreeing with the child's expressed ideas, we are providing further stimulus to continue growth in understandings. If we also explain the basis for our agreement, we further feed thinking by modeling the process of checking. For example, when a child who is manipulating geometric shapes exclaims, "Look! I made a square with these pieces." validation takes the form of "Yes. I see your square—with four sides, all the same length."

Reviewing serves to strengthen skills and clarify understandings. As the mathematics education community shifts the focus of teaching from mastering skills to developing understandings, the related teaching strategies have simultaneously shifted from an emphasis on drill and practice to interactive discussions about children's emerging ideas and understandings. For example, when a child has figured out how many apples are needed for a planned cooking activity, reviewing takes the form of "How did you figure that out?"

Challenging extends children's consideration of mathematical relationships. It can stimulate thinking without additional manipulation of the materials or can propel further action with the materials by involving more complex thinking. For example, when a child figures out how many strips of precut paper are needed to frame a picture for a bulletin board, challenging in order to extend children's thinking may take the form of saying, "I wonder how many strips you would need if your strips were half of that size." Challenging to stimulate further action may take the form of saying, "I think we have an additional picture to frame. How many more strips are you going to need?"

Selecting the Appropriate Instructional Strategy

Choices

Making a selection from one of the three strategies, validating, reviewing, or extending and challenging, is not as easy as it may seem. It requires (1) an awareness of how the mathematical aspects of the child's thinking fit on the curriculum maps discussed in Chapters 4 and 5, and (2) knowledge of the child's learning style and interests at the moment. Coordinating the observational information with the curriculum map allows the adult to "catch them thinking mathematics." That is our cue to swing into action. The dilemma arises as we make a selection from the possible routes to pursue.

Prekindergarten Opportunities

The following vignette occurred in a prekindergarten class.

Mark, who just turned four, was organizing a collection of animal figures from a large Lego set. He lined up the animals on the floor, two by two. After pairing five sets, he picked up a lion, looked at the collection, and declared, "Hey, a lion is missing." He searched through the Lego blocks still in the box, and upon finding another lion, he completed the pairing and declared, "There you are!" Once he finished this task he had set for himself, he pointed to each pair and quietly counted, "One, two. One, two. . . ." Next, he called to the teacher, "Look. I have two, and two and two and two. . . ." as he pointed to each pair.

How does one respond to this moment of "thinking mathematically"? If we want to build on Mark's ideas, we have to tune into what is important to him in this event. He is connecting his fascination with pairing by organizing the set of animals. In the mathematics education literature, this is called "knowing what the number two means." We also need to tune into his level of knowing. Clearly, he knows the difference between a set of one and a set of two.

Counting is his tool. In thinking about our choices for interaction,

1. We could validate Mark's thinking, by agreeing with him that he has "lots of sets of two animals" and labeling the sets with him, saying, "You have two lions, and two elephants and two dogs and two

goats . . ." An additional point of validation could include a comment about his search through the materials to complete the set of lions: "I watched you looking for the other lion, so you would have two of them in your collection." This is a viable option because it does not change the course of Mark's thinking and it allows him to select the next step in the talk or action. However, if he has run out of ideas, it fails to stimulate further action.

2. We could review, by asking him to show you again, for example, "What do you mean, two and two and two? Will you show me?" This approach calls for a repeat of action and allows Mark to add to the initial statement, identifying the similarity of sets of two, irrespective of the elements in the sets, that is, generalizing about "twoness." Once again, this strategy does not necessarily provoke further action.

3. We could extend Mark's mathematical thinking, without additional manipulation. This might feature counting that leads to simple computation, such as, "How many sets do you have in all?" followed by, "How many animals are there all together?" If Mark is challenged by notions of "how many altogether," this strategy may spark a whole new set of investigations about mathematical relationships. If he is not interested, he may turn away.

4. We could extend Mark's mathematical thinking through action and capitalize on his interests in dramatic play. Engaging him in conversation about the feeding or sleeping needs of the animals introduces a context in which to find out if there are enough Lego pieces for each set of animals to have its own "feeding" or "sleeping" area. This may provoke an exploration of the mathematical relationship of two-to-one or many-to-one, or it may spark a totally new avenue of investigation, such as *area*. "Can all the pairs fit within the same area created with the blocks?" Props, such as fences to construct feeding pens, provide many options for exploration of mathematical relationships in number, geometry, and measurement.

Kindergarten Opportunities

In the following vignette we can "catch them thinking mathematics."

Richard and Andre, who regularly enjoy working together in the block area, were jointly constructing railroad tracks. Richard was using all lengths of blocks: units, double units, longs, and double longs. Andre was using only one size, the long size. When the tracks were approximately three feet long, an argument erupted. Each time Andre placed a block along his side of the road, Richard took it away, declaring firmly, "No." This argument escalated into a more heated exchange. When the teacher inquired about the problem, Richard complained that Andre was spoiling the tracks, and Andre countered with a protest that Richard keeps taking his blocks.

In this situation, adults are prone to adopt a conflict resolution approach to deal with the children's expressed emotional frustrations. "What's the problem? Richard, is that true? Did you take Andre's blocks? Why did you take his blocks? If you think he is spoiling the roadway, you need to talk to him about it." However, needs of the youngsters might well be better served through teacher responses that focus on the process of children's mathematical thinking during the event that probably accounts for the conflict.

1. The use of the validation strategy is very limited. Since the children did not verbally declare their mathematical thinking, the adult is required to interpret from observation. "It looks like you were making your tracks differently." If this provokes explanations about how they perceived the construction task, then the adult can validate the two different ways they viewed the linear array. If it turns out that Richard was concerned with the length of the tracks, irrespective of the length of the blocks, while Andre was concerned with matching blocks by size, again both approaches can be validated. Once validated, the problem of how to resolve these differences serves to extend thinking and action.

2. Reviewing the plans for and the decisions made by the two boys provides an opportunity to expose different mathematical concerns, such as building for length, building for equivalent length, creating parallel lines, or using a specific number of blocks.

   The teacher might ask, "When you started, did you discuss what size blocks to use or how long the tracks would be?" "Let's take a look at the two sides of the tracks and see how they are the same and how they are different," or "Richard, does Andre's side of the tracks look the way you expected it to?" and asking the reverse question of Andre. Review questions can expose differences in the mathematical lens being used by the two boys and ultimately extend thinking.

3. Extending options depends upon successful review of differences in each boy's approach. The problem-resolution approach engages the child in figuring out how to construct the track in ways that the builders mutually agree upon. It might take the form of using identical lengths at each step in the process, such as one unit block on each side, then one long block, or ending with sides of equal length irrespective of the lengths of the blocks used in order to construct the opposite sides. The differences in mathematical thinking reflected in this event create a context for the adult to serve both cognitive and social–emotional goals. The cognitive goal centers on clarifying and extending thinking. The social–emotional goal centers on negotiating conflict and supporting self-esteem.

Many of the disputes that arise in the classroom of young children grow out of differences in points of view. The premise forwarded here is that children's self-esteem is often better served through helping them work through differences in ideas and perceptions than in focusing on the emotional responses produced when conflicting ideas interrupt an activity. Similarly, instructional strategies that coordinate with children's mathematical thinking, rather than judgmental evaluations, help children to value their own work.

Hidden Messages in Teacher Talk: Praise and Empowerment

Teaching responses such as "Good," "Great," "How smart you are," and "That's wonderful" are examples of value judgments, externally imposed.[2] These statements of praise lack any focus on content or children's thinking and thus tend to derail further conversation. Instead, the child is placed in a position of looking for ways to obtain more praise without a clue as to what content or idea provoked the adult praise. In order to increase effectiveness in fostering thinking, it is necessary to sort out the kinds of adult talk that supports the process from that which gets in the way.

Take, for example, the following two classroom observations in which the adult response was limited to a brief comment of praise.

Tressa had just completed assembling a geometric jigsaw puzzle with triangles, squares, and circles of different sizes and was sharing her accomplishment with her prekindergarten teacher. "Look, look. I finished." The teacher smiled and commented enthusiastically, "Good job!"

A mathematical content response could have used any of the three strategies discussed above. Validation: "Yes. I can see. You found a space for each shape. There are no shapes left and no empty spaces." Review: "Let's name the shapes you put into the puzzle." Extension: "Yes. Let's see how many shapes you put into the puzzle." This might lead to counting all the shape pieces, and then finding out how many of each shape are in the puzzle.

> In response to his kindergarten teacher's question about how many crackers he needed for the four children in his table group, if each child is to have two crackers, Lee declared, "8 crackers." The teacher declared warmly, "Good thinking."

Mathematical content responses for this event might take these forms:

> *Validate*: "Sounds OK to me. Why don't you check to see if you have the right number for each person to have two crackers?"
>
> *Review*: "That was fast. How did you figure that out?"
>
> *Extend*: "If we decided to give each person three crackers, how many would you need to take?"

For each child in the above vignettes, the suggested conversation reflects a valuing of their thinking by validating, reviewing, or extending what they were thinking about during the activity.

A Case for Limiting Praise

It is common practice to use everyday expressions of praise in early childhood classrooms where we strongly value helping children feel good about themselves. When adults praise young children, they are assuming children need this kind of feedback in order to value what they have done and assuming they will not appreciate the importance of their accomplishments without adult praise. This is certainly true in the development of values and social skills associated with caring about the welfare of others and taking responsibility as a member of a family or social group. The socialization process requires informing children about the acceptable and unacceptable behaviors of the social group within which the child is growing up. In this sense, praise with justification supports the children's sense of belonging as they adapt their own behavior to the group code.

However, praise supporting children's self-valuing does not necessarily serve the development of academic autonomy or empower children as thinkers and doers (Kamii & Housman 2000). It often seems to achieve just the opposite effect. Praise comments like "good job," "good thinking," "beautiful," "lovely," and "nice" in the above vignettes carry two different kinds of messages. One message we want to send is that the adult values children's actions or products; the second message—one we do not want to send—is that the adult is always passing judgment on children's work and without adult approval children will not know the value of their accomplishments or even know if they have "done well." One perspective views this practice as creating "praise junkies" who cannot live without the adult praise (Kohn 2001).

Over the past decade the educational community has expressed increased concern for developing instructional strategies that shift the emphasis from extrinsic rewards provided by others to intrinsic rewards fed by internal values. Publications from NCTM highlight concerns about the results of the product-focused and answer-oriented teaching approach. One of the five major shifts in *Professional Standards for Teaching Mathematics* is toward logic and mathematical reasoning and away from the teacher as the sole authority for right answers (NCTM 1991). Translating this goal into the communication between adults and young children poses some challenging decisions centering on *when* and *where* to use verbal praise.

Young children continually seek to share their discoveries and accomplishments with adults. We do not want to withhold approval at the price of making children worry about whether they are succeeding. On the other hand, if we take a different perspective, we may discover that the sharing they do is not so much for approval as for seeking genuine interaction with us about their experiences. In the following kindergarten vignette, there is a strong indication that the child was seeking something more than generalized praise.

Joshua had just completed his collage of a boat scene. He raised his finished product in the air and studied it, smiling and nodding. In the background could be heard the teacher responding to children's work. "Lovely, Janie." "Great, Pedro." "Sondra, how beautiful!" "Nice picture Alonzo." After studying the results, Joshua turned and began skipping toward the teacher. Halfway there, he stopped, looked at her, listened for a few seconds, and then turned away, no longer smiling. He walked to the product storage shelf, left his picture, and somberly walked away.

Joshua's behavior provokes thoughts about the kinds of teacher comments that would have kept him coming to her. Instead of the nonspecific judgmental terms "beautiful," "lovely," and "nice," other choices include

- validating—commenting on elements of the picture that focus on size comparisons ("I see you put two boats in your picture. One is bigger than the other. Did you plan it that way?");
- reviewing—focusing on shape comparisons and ordinal sequence ("This boat has one sail. Have you ever seen [ridden in] a boat like this?" "Which ship did you paste first? And then what did you paste next . . . last?"); or
- extending—thinking about distance and volume ("How many people can ride in your boat?" "Are these ships traveling very far?" "Do they carry the same number of people?")—or classification for creating sets ("How is your boat different than the one in the story about 'Little Toot' that we read yesterday?" "Let's look at that boat magazine I brought in last week. I wonder what other kinds of boats there are besides sailboats.").

Comments that extend conversation relating directly to children's responses set the context for the next project, which might be making a wooden boat or experimenting with the movement of boats at the water table.

Matching Instructional Strategies with the Learning in Progress

As discussed in Chapter 6, mathematical learning in early childhood environments generally shows up in three forms that include (1) making mathematical discoveries, (2) repetitive use of emerging mathematical skills, and (3) applying mathematical skills and understanding. It is important to identify the difference in response formats which empower children mathematically and foster cognitive autonomy in these three different forms of learning.

Making Discoveries. Teaching messages that empower children to continue discovering are ones that value revisiting the discovery. This value is communicated through encouraging repeated trials and further experimentation to validate initial findings (Kamii & DeVries 1978; Wassermann 1990). For example, when a child discovers a relationship between two events, adult language that encourages revisiting the events for further discovery involves the use of such phrases as "I wonder . . . do you suppose . . . if you counted the five blocks on one side of your building and the five on the other side again would it still come out the same, ten blocks?" (*validating*), or "Do you think that . . . if you took another ten blocks, you could make another building just like this one?" (*building generalizations*) After working at the task, a further revisiting is achieved through an invitation to identify how the child approaches the task.

The first thrust encourages revisiting to validate, while the second one serves to test the discovery under a separate condition. The second approach also may lead to extending discovery by inviting the child to find out if she could construct a similar building with different-sized blocks or use ten more blocks on the same structure to discover how it changes. Ultimately, revisiting the experience to examine the process supports thinking about how the result was achieved and equips the child to repeat and extend the mathematical learnings in the next endeavor. While praise may also provoke repeated constructions, the focus of such effort is more likely to recreate the structure which the adult judged "very good."

The adult can transmit the same messages by responding to children's work during a planned curriculum activity. For example, when children discover that they can create a square by arranging two triangles in a particular way, the phrases "I wonder . . . ," "Do you suppose . . . ," or "See if . . ." serve as an invitation to compare the outcomes. This approach can support the development of a sense of a community of discoverers.

Practicing Skills. Young children are perpetually practicing mathematical skills that capture their interest. They count and recount. They repeatedly create shapes. They copy, repeat, and extend patterns. The primary purpose of practice is to achieve accuracy and speed. When children take pride in their growing mathematical skills, the temptation to praise is very great. Yet, the message that we want to communicate is one of sharing satisfaction and supporting further practice through revisiting the speed and accuracy of the skill. For example, youngsters often spontaneously speed-count, by ones, twos, fives, or tens. The invitation to revisit can take the form of finding out about speed and accuracy:

"I wonder if you can count as high when counting by twos as by tens."

"Do you suppose you can get to 100 faster counting by twos or by tens?"

"Do you find that you lose your place with the numbers when you count really fast?"

"Does it make a difference whether you whisper or talk out loud when you are counting by tens?"

Applying Skills and Understandings. In prekindergarten and kindergarten classes, children continually apply their mathematical knowledge and skills in interest-center activities. It is much easier to support children's mathematical progress in activities that they choose. Application experiences offer the most opportunities to communicate a valuing of thinking as children plan, test, and evaluate their work related to expected outcomes.

When children seek to share their completed products, there are several ways to help the child revisit the mathematical problem solving that occurred during construction. One starting point for conversation helps the child think about whether the finished work was the intended product:

- When you started this project, did you plan to make this mobile look like this?
- If not, how is it different from what you planned?
- Why did you change your plans?

A different thrust for conversation revisits the mathematical thinking and problem solving in which the child engaged:

- How did you get this to balance? That certainly looks like it was not easy to do.
- Did you have any problems making the pieces fit? What kind? How did you solve them?
- If you were to make another one, would it be the same or different? In what way?

Both conversational routes engage the child in talking about the ideas used in the process of completing the project and open up opportunities to identify some of the mathematics embedded in the tasks.

A Case for Process-Oriented Questions and Responses in Group Interactions

The greatest challenge to avoid the hidden messages which place primary value on correct answers occurs during teacher-directed activities. Group time, with its management demands, seems to create the context in which the tradition of questioning to elicit accurate responses tends to dominate teaching strategies. The use of fact-focused questions that begin with "Who knows . . . ?" "Who can tell me . . . ?" or "Who remembers . . . ?" are often followed with value-laden responses, "Good," "Great answer," "Almost right," and "Who can help her?" These teaching strategies associated with direct instruction are intended to maintain a pace and avoid distracting behavior by the children. However, they frequently achieve the opposite result. The rapid responders eagerly participate and those who do not feel that they can respond have trouble maintaining focus.

Provoking thinking with large groups is more challenging then with individual children. However, the same questioning approach applies. Thought-provoking questions that feature figuring out patterns and relationships shift children's attention to the content of the activity rather than earning praise from the adult. For example, when telling a tangram or geometry shape story using flannel board cutouts, a process-oriented question is, "What shapes do you think we could use to make this next shape in the story?" This question sets the stage for an action response: "Let's try it and see what happens." It further provides for trying out more ideas: "What other shapes could we try?" These thinking questions stand in stark contrast to "Who knows what two shapes we need to make this triangle?"—a question that relies primarily on memorized information.

Revisiting the construction of the shape can occur whether the first solution was accurate or not. If it did not work, the question "What's wrong with this shape we created?" serves to challenge thinking. As children compare the product with the intended shape, a natural follow-up is to figure out what kind of shapes to try next. If the first solution worked, a challenge to find other options extends the search.

Adapting Instructional Strategies. When working with a whole class of children, it is important to use strategies that hold their attention. The most frequently used strategies are to ask questions that children can answer easily. Within this pattern, interactions tend to be answer oriented and brief. However, other possibilities exist. Questions can emphasize ways to think about and figure out answers rather than expect children to have the answers.

Take, for example, the following two vignettes. In the first vignette, the adult is reading a counting book to a class of preprimary children. The typical pattern reinforces counting practice, primarily by one child. The attention of the rest of the group on the precision of counting is unpredictable. The optional pattern features the idea that the order in which a set is counted does not change the size of the set. Counting practice is embedded in the task.

The teacher and children were gathered in a group looking at a beautifully illustrated counting book. The purpose of the activity was to strengthen the children's counting skills and their ability to associate numbers with sets.

Typical Pattern	**Optional Pattern**
As the teacher shared the book with the children she asked, "Who can show me how many seagulls there are on this page?" The teacher selected a counter for each page from the eager volunteers.	Invitation to count: "Let's check to see how many seagulls are on this page. Where shall we begin?" Choosing a helper: invite one child to count. Invitation to check: "Let's see if we get the same number if we start with a different seagull." Choosing a different helper.

In the second vignette, the teacher is engaging the children in preparing for a trip.

The teacher and children were planning for a trip to a local park.

Typical Pattern Focuses on Answers	**Optional Pattern Focuses on Figuring Out**
As the teacher guided the planning discussion she asked such questions as "Who knows how many milk cartons we will need for the trip?" followed by, "Tell me how you know this?"	Figuring out how to approach the mathematical task: "What do you suppose we need to know in order to figure out how many milk cartons to take? What else do we need to go with the milk cartons?" Thinking about how to approach a computational task: "How will we

figure how many crackers to take,
in order for everyone to have 4?"
Engaging children in the task:
Assign groups to figure it out their
own way. Compare computational
strategies of the groups as well as the
answers.

The typical pattern in this vignette again features "knowing the answer,"
followed by an explanation of how one knows the answer. The optional
pattern places emphasis on what information children need in order to
answer a mathematical question. No computation is involved in the first
question, unless visitors are expected. These two different approaches to
solving the problem can be summarized as follows:

Valuing Answers	Valuing Thinking on the Way to Answers
Emphasis on knowing and producing the right answer	Emphasis on figuring out
Emphasis on being the first to produce the answer	Emphasis on taking the time to figure it out
Emphasis of adult verification of answer	Emphasis on testing ideas and checking
Emphasis on a single computational procedure	Emphasis on multiple routes to compute and answer
Emphasis on adult praise	Emphasis on intrinsic valuing of own thinking
Emphasis on personal gain from individual effort	Emphasis on sharing thinking and group effort

Table 7.1 illustrates ways to transform adult praise from a generalized
valuing of the person to teaching responses that carry the message of
valuing the process of thinking and figuring-out problems. When the
communication climate changes, children also change the way they address learning challenges for themselves and with each other.

Impact on Children. When a kindergarten teacher altered her pattern of
response from praise to content-based responses, she realized that she was
communicating more enthusiasm for the child's work by engaging in a
conversation rather than just offering praise. She reported the following
interchange that had occurred after a child had completed a construction:

Table 7.1
Transforming Teaching Messages from Extrinsic Rewards to Extending Thinking

Learning Context	Extrinsic Rewards Providing Praise and Retaining Control	Intrinsic Valuing of the Process Extending Children's Thinking
Discovering Relationships	"Great." "Aren't you smart?"	**Revisit the process**: "I wonder if the same thing would happen if you tried it again."
	"Wonderful." "Beautiful."	**Review the thinking**: "How did you discover that?"
	"Show me how else you can do it."	**Test under different conditions**: "Do you suppose that it would also work with other materials?"
	"Everybody. Look what a good job A. did. Who else did a good job like this?"	**Check and compare**: "Why don't you check with J——to see if she made it the same way you did."
Practicing Skills	"You're very fast." "Great counting." "Wow, are you good at counting!"	**Alter the task**: "I wonder if you counted by twos instead of ones whether it would take more, less, or the same amount of time."
	"Who can count these birds for us (me)?" "Who else can do it?"	**Focus on the process rather than the person**: "Where shall we start counting?"
	"Right."	**Test a mathematical concept**: "If we started with a different bird, would there still be the same number of birds on this page?"
Applying Skills and Understandings during Group Time	"Who knows . . . ?" "Who can tell me . . . ?" "Good answer." "Good thinking." "What a great mobile you made."	**Examine possibilities**: "Let's see what shapes we might use to create a triangle. How did it work? What other shapes might also fit together to make a triangle?"

John pointed to a tower he had built out of Legos for his mom. He told me that it was an apartment building. Instead of saying something like "Wow. Your mom is going to love the way it is so tall" (which I would have said two days ago!), instead, I said, "Now, when you decided to build something, did you know you were going to be building an apartment building?" His eyes lit up as he answered. I was shocked to see how excited he was that I was interested in his creation. If I had followed my usual pattern of just making a comment on it, our conversation would have been over. By commenting on it the way I did, however, our conversation was only beginning. John proceeded to tell me that he wanted to build a house but that the building started to look more like an apartment building so he changed his mind. I asked him what he would have done differently if he had decided to stick to his original plan and build a house. He showed me with the Legos, explaining as he did so. Then he actually decided to build the house and together we compared the house with the apartment building.

What we learn from authentic conversations with children is the potential depth of their thinking and capabilities for transforming understanding into action.

Concluding Remarks

If we are to realize the goal of empowering the learner in mathematics, we are challenged to systematically explore teacher talk. One critical goal at the heart of quality interactions is fostering intellectual autonomy in the learner. This requires that the adult distinguish between those comments and questions that unwittingly encourage dependency upon the authority figure and those that support the growth of academic autonomy. The former transfers the basis of evaluation of a child's thinking or action from the child to the adult; the latter, those that empower the child to pursue inquiry, skill development, and problem solving, help the child revisit and extend a learning experience. Authentic discussions serve the long-term goal of empowering children as thinkers.

Authentic conversation with children has its origins in curriculum content. The next set of chapters examine the ways that mathematics intersects with curriculum topics and subject areas. Chapter 8 features time recording tools, followed by chapters in the curriculum areas of science and social studies.

Notes

1. This section is adapted from Schwartz, S. L., & Brown, A. E. (1995), "Communicating with young children in mathematics: A unique challenge," *Teaching Children Mathematics* 1 (6): 250–254. Reprinted with permission from *Teaching Children Mathematics*, © by the National Council of Teachers of Mathematics. All rights reserved.

2. This section is adapted from Schwartz, S. L. (1996), "Hidden messages in teacher talk: Praise and empowerment," *Teaching Children Mathematics* 2 (7): 396–401. Reprinted with permission from *Teaching Children Mathematics*, © by the National Council of Teachers of Mathematics. All rights reserved.

References

Capps, L., & Pickreign, J. (1993). "Language connections in mathematics: A critical part of mathematics instruction." *Arithmetic Teacher* (Sept. 1993): 8–12.

Carpenter, T., Fennema, E., Franke, M., Levi, L., & Empson, S. (1999). *Children's mathematics: Cognitively guided instruction*. Portsmouth, NH: Heinemann.

Curcio, F. R., Schwartz, S. L., & Brown, C. A. (1996). "Developing preservice teachers' strategies for communicating in and about mathematics." In Elliott, P., & Kenney, M. (Eds.), *Communication in mathematics, K–12 and beyond*, pp. 204–214. 1996 Yearbook of National Council of Teachers of Mathematics (NCTM). Reston, VA: NCTM.

Dacey, L. S., & Easton, R. (1999). *Growing mathematical ideas in the kindergarten*. Sausalito, CA: Math Solutions Publications.

Fosnot, C. T., & Dolk, M. (2001). *Young mathematicians at work: Constructing number sense, addition, and subtraction*. Portsmouth, NH: Heinemann.

Ginsberg, H., Inoue N., & Seo, K. (1999). "Young children doing mathematics: Observations of everyday activities." In Copley, J. (Ed.), *Mathematics in the early years*, pp. 88–101. Washington, DC: National Association for the Education of Young Children.

Greenberg, P. (1993). "How and why to teach all aspects of preschool and kindergarten math naturally, democratically, and effectively." Part 1, *Young Children* 48 (4): 75–84; Part 2, *Young Children* 49 (2): 12–18.

Kamii, C., & DeVries, R. (1978). *Physical knowledge in preschool education: Implications of Piaget's theory*. Englewood Cliffs, NJ: Prentice Hall.

Kamii, C., & Housman, L. (2000). *Young children reinvent arithmetic*. 2nd ed. New York: Teachers College Press.

Kamii, C., & Joseph, L. (1982). *Number in preschool and kindergarten: Educational Implications of Piaget's theory*. Washington, DC: National Association for the Education of Young Children.

Katz, L., & Chard, S. (2000). *Engaging children's minds: The project approach*. 2nd ed. Norwood, NJ: Ablex.

Kohn, A. (2001). "Five reasons to stop saying 'Good job!' " *Young Children* (Sept. 2000): 24–29.

National Council of Teachers of Mathematics (NCTM). (1989). *Curriculum and evaluation standards for school mathematics.* Reston, VA: NCTM.

———. (1991). *Professional standards for teaching mathematics.* Reston, VA: NCTM.

Rowe, M. B. (1986). "Wait time: Slowing down may be a way of speeding up!" *Journal of Teacher Education* 37 (January/February): 43–50.

Schwartz, S. L. (1996). "Hidden messages in teacher talk: Praise and empowerment." *Teaching Children Mathematics* 2 (7): 396–401.

Schwartz, S. L., & Brown, A. E. (1995). "Communicating with young children in mathematics: A unique challenge." *Teaching Children Mathematics* 1 (6): 26–28.

Wassermann, S. (1990). *Serious players in the primary classroom: Empowering children through active learning experiences.* New York: Teachers College Press.

CHAPTER 8

Calendars and Clocks

Tools for Time Management

Ronny: I hurt my leg—tomorrow—no—yesterday on the sidewalk.
Teacher: What is the difference between yesterday and tomorrow?
Ronny: Yesterday is gone. Tomorrow did not come yet.
Conversation recorded between a four-year-old boy and his teacher.
(Wann 1962, 48)

The daily lives of children provoke continual thinking about the sequence of their experiences. They engage in looking ahead as well as looking back, as Ronny so precisely demonstrates.[1]

Time-recording devices in the hands of children can serve as authentic tools to serve curriculum while children engage in repeated use of mathematical skills and strategies. These tools for recording and keeping track of important events in the lives of children help them orient themselves in past, present, and future time. In order to achieve this goal with preprimary children it is essential to design a tool that they can use to record and refer to events that are important to them. At first, young children can focus of their daily schedule. Ultimately, they want to increase their knowledge about the schedules they will need to plan and follow.

The Conventional Approach

In early childhood, the use of individual calendars by children can serve one of our critical goals of engaging children as partners in the teaching–learning environment. With experience, the calendar and clock can become powerful tools for primary children to keep records of their experiences, to identify patterns and relationships of time–event experiences, and to take increasing responsibility for both their school and home lives through planning. Our challenge is to change the conventional approach so that children can become active users of the tools.

The Transmission Approach to Reading the Calendar

> It was the middle of March and the prekindergarten class had gathered for the beginning activities of the day. In a familiar sequence, the program proceeded from attendance taking to calendar reading. The teacher focused children's attention on the calendar, pointing to the X marked in the calendar matrix. "Yesterday was Tuesday. Who knows what today is?" Several different responses emanated from the group. Among them was "Wednesday." After verifying, "Yes. Today is Wednesday," the teacher pointed to the previous day's date, stating "Yesterday was the twenty-second. What is today's date?" There was no response. The teacher called on one child to come up and point to the number of today's date. When the child was unable to read the number, the teacher prompted by pointing to the numeral 2, asking the child to read it. Then she repeated the question pointing to the numeral 3. After repeating the names of the numerals 2 and 3 several times she provided the children with a rule: "Whenever you have a 2 and a 3, you have 23." This calendar reading activity closed with the teacher's summary, "Today is Wednesday, March 23rd."

The problems that surround this typical mechanistic approach to calendar reading can be best understood in the context of the mathematical relationships involved in the task. From a mathematical perspective, successful reading of a calendar requires an initial understanding of a matrix that has five or more rows with seven cells in each row. Take, for example, the March calendar used in the above vignette (see Table 8.1).

Table 8.1
March Calendar

Sunday	Monday	Tuesday	Wednesday	Thursday	Friday	Saturday
		1	2	3	4	5
6	7	8	9	10	11	12
13	14	15	16	17	18	19
20	21	22	23	24	25	26
27	28	29	30	31		

The first row has day labels in every cell beginning with Sunday. In the next row the notation in the cells changes from words to numerals. Not all the cells in the first and last row have numerals, although once the first numeral is entered, the rest follow in reading order, left to right and up to down. The location of the numeral 1 on the first row of written numbers changes from month to month. What the children see is two charts with lines of boxes or cells, some of which have entries and others of which do not.

Additional problems can be understood as we take a developmental perspective. Preprimary children often do not accurately count to thirty-one, much less read double-digit numerals. They have a great deal of difficulty making sense out of a five-row, seven-column matrix. Complicating this task are such factors as (1) different ending numbers on each month's chart, sometimes 30 and sometimes 31 with no predictable pattern, (2) interchanging of the cardinal number and ordinal number, for example, twenty-three and twenty-third, (3) connecting the X- and Y-axis for day and date information, and (4) reading the counting numbers up to thirty-one. Although most kindergarten children can ultimately master the task of locating day and date, there is little or no use for this information either in their school or home lives. If we are going to take the time to focus on the calendar, it makes sense to think in terms of its primary function and then design experiences that can fulfill this function for children.

Commercial Curriculum Approach to Reading the Calendar

Some curriculum publishers have recently designed a variety of programs that use the school calendar-reading event to teach a variety of mathematical skills not necessarily a part of calendar reading, such as interval counting by tens and using colors to distinguish odd and even numbers. Each one of these skills is important, but is not necessarily well connected to the calendar format. Table 8.2 illustrates the contradictions or problems that arise when teachers use the calendar to teach relationships that do not readily fit the seven-by-five matrix of the monthly formats.

Although these newly designed curriculum programs provide a more attractive context for pursuing the traditional mathematics curriculum than the conventional worksheet-dependent skill-drill programs, they do not provide a meaningful form of learning for young children.

Table 8.2
Problems with Some Commercial Calendar-Reading Programs

Mathematical Skill Prescribed	Problem
Interval counting by tens: clustering sticks or chips into sets of ten to keep track of elapsed days of the month or year.	Overrides the concept of a seven-day week.
Linear patterning: featured by imposing a color or shape pattern on the calendar grid.	Ignores the calendar information and instead requires focus on the color-shape pattern.
Matching number names to numerals.	Lack of familiarity with the number sequence up to 31 limits recognition of written double-digit numbers.
Coordinating cardinal number and ordinal number, e.g., day # 3 or the 3rd day.	Beginning counters become confused by the switch from the use of counting numbers and numerals to ordinal numbers designating position in a number sequence.

How to Make Calendars Meaningful

The development of calendar activities unfolds in a very different way if we start with children's concerns. The primary function of calendars for adults is essentially one of organization. We use them to organize our schedules, to plan for present and future time—today and tomorrow. A secondary function is to keep a record of past time to serve as a resource for current planning. In essence, the calendar is a tool for schedule planning and review. Our task is to develop calendar experiences so that it serves children in the same way it serves adults.

Young children are very concerned with event sequences in their daily and weekly lives. They endlessly ask, "When are we gonna' . . . ?" Thus, a natural starting point is the introduction of a format for helping them find answers to that refrain of "When are we gonna'?" They need to have access to some kind of a written record of activity sequences that they can use to anticipate desired events.

Events which traditionally surround calendar discussion in most preprimary and primary classrooms include those which repeat yearly— the seasons, holidays, family rituals, and birthdays. However, events spaced at such great distances in time do not offer young children fundamental experiences for developing time concepts. In the lives of four-, five-, or six-year-old children, the distance from one winter to the next, or one Thanksgiving to the next, constitutes one-quarter to one-sixth of their whole life. Sequencing based on such long intervals requires a more advanced development of time concepts than that attained by young children. Mastery of time concepts grows from immediate sequences of events with intervals of minutes, hours, and days rather then months and years. Simple time intervals encompass a day, or perhaps yesterday-today-tomorrow.

The fact that there are problems with using the conventional approach to teaching children about calendars does not mean that we need to abandon the idea of "calendaring" activities with children. In fact, quite the reverse is true. The children let us know, in no uncertain terms, that they want to be able to know what is coming and when. They continue to turn to the adult because the adult calendar does not reveal the answers they seek such as, "When are we going to visit the farm?" "Is the music teacher coming today?" "How many days before my birthday party?" Similarly, past events capture their attention, although not necessarily in accurate order of time intervals. "Remember yesterday when I got my new coat?" "I remember yesterday when you hurt your foot." *Yesterday* refers to time past and could mean anytime from yesterday to weeks or months ago.

An examination of children's development of time concepts provides a window into designing time-recording experiences that will contribute to children's emerging abilities to orient themselves in past, present, and future time.

Development of Time Concepts

Initially, concepts of time consist of "now time" and "not-now time." Babies react to what is in the present, and they have little to do with what is *not* occurring at the moment. Awareness of "not-now time" grows through the process of recognizing the relationship between events, such as when the feeding adult appears in response to a baby's hunger cry. Soon, with repeated experiences, "not-now time" is sorted into two frames, "past time" and "future time." For example, the baby stops crying upon the appearance of the feeding adult, even before food is offered. The baby's recall of prior experiences of the sequence of events for feeding serves to establish anticipation of response to the call for food. Finally, as children progress through infancy and toddlerhood into the early childhood years, having many repeated experiences of daily living and special events, they begin to order in sequence the important events that have already occurred and to plan the sequence of future events. By the time young children enter prekindergarten, we have convincing evidence that, although they may misuse the language labels *yesterday* and *tomorrow*, they understand the difference between past time and future time (Wann et al. 1962). The process of understanding the relationship between past and present events establishes the foundation for children to become active agents in planning for future events. Data-recording systems can serve as one tool to help meet this challenge.

Developing Event-Recording Systems

In a very real sense, children begin constructing their own informal calendars as they recall events that happened in the past and anticipate and plan future events. Children who can use their knowledge of prior experiences over a period of time become empowered to plan for and adapt to future events. Our task is to support this emerging awareness of time in order to provide the kind of tools they can use to bridge between what they already know and the development of their time concepts. By constructing recording forms with children, we can feed this process of making connections between past, present, and future events that reflect their activity interests.

Early childhood teachers with whom I have worked over the past thirty years generated the following ideas. Many sessions were devoted to thinking through the reasons for and possibilities of designing event-recording experiences that young children could use as useful tools as well as facilitating management within the program.

Constructing Calendars with Preprimary Children

Preprimary teachers consistently identify two major uses for time-recording tools. One is to make a public record of recurring daily events for children's reference. The other is to plan future events so that necessary preparations can be made in a timely way.

A Daily Schedule of Events. When we discussed approaches to recording events with young children, the teachers reported that children were very unstable in their orientation to the sequence of the daily activities at the beginning of the program. It became increasingly clear that the first teaching task was to help children master the sequence of a single day before looking at a span of days. Although a daily schedule does not conform to adult notions of a calendar, in fact, the first kind of event record

Table 8.3
Daily Schedule: Horizontal Format

Center Time	Snack Time	Circle Time	Story Time	Outdoor Time
Pictures of objects in the centers	Pictures or paste-ups of straws, napkins, or other snack materials	A circle of faces including the teacher	Picture or miniature book	Pictures of outdoor equipment and materials

that young children seek is one that helps them deal comfortably with immediate periods of time. In preprimary as well as primary programs, this constitutes one day's events. To meet this need, teachers of nonreaders devised simple daily schedule charts using picture symbols to designate each of the periods which occurred regularly in the daily program (Table 8.3). Sometimes written labels were also included. When children asked such questions as, "When are we going to have snack?" the chart served as a reference for teachers and children together. "We are having center time now. Let's look at our schedule to see what comes next, and where snack time is on the schedule." Soon, children began to use the posted daily schedule to answer their own questions without addressing them to the teacher first.

As the teachers shared their daily schedule charts with each other, they agreed that the style of the chart was not the important factor, as long as it served the function of facilitating the development of the children's understanding of event sequences. Whether they used drawings, cutouts, or three-dimensional objects was a matter of teacher choice. Both horizontal and vertical representations (Table 8.3 and Table 8.4) were used.

The value of the *vertical* representation is that it distinguishes a daily schedule governed by the passage of time in hours, from a weekly schedule governed by passage of time in days. The value of the *horizontal* format is that it launches children immediately into a left-to-right reading modality from the first experience with event-recording systems. Either way, children engage in thinking about positional terms such as *next to*, *before, after,* and *in-between,* as well as ordering the set of daily activities in a repeated sequence.

Primary programs housed in larger institutional settings depend more upon a variety of factors that determine each day's schedule. Neverthe-

Table 8.4
Daily Schedule: Vertical Format

Center Time

Pictures of objects in the centers

Snack Time

Pictures or paste-ups of straws, napkins, or other snack materials

Circle Time

A circle of faces including the teacher

Story Time

Picture or miniature book

Outdoor Time

Pictures of outdoor equipment and materials

less, primary-grade children can only develop a sense of control and responsibility over their actions if they know the schedule that will govern
their day. In this way they can anticipate what will be expected of them
during the different segments of the program.

Additional activities to support this introduction to clock reading took
the form of having children, with the help of their parents, draw a picture
of the placement of the hands on the clock at critical moments in their day,
such as when they get up in the morning or when they leave for school.

A Weekly Schedule of Events. Once children tuned into the pattern of
a single day's schedule, the teachers identified opportunities to work with
children to create a weekly schedule. For example, in one school setting,
the prekindergarten children had access to the school gymnasium once a
week, and children needed to bring their sneakers for that event. In another school setting, the children had a music period twice a week. Teachers noted that the children continually sought to identify the time
sequences that explained the order of these special events. "Do we have
gym today?" "Do I need to bring my sneakers tomorrow?" "When are
we going to have music?"

Acting on these observations, teachers designed calendars to answer
children's questions. The first weekly event-recording system noted special
events that occurred only once or twice weekly. For those days on which
there was no special event, the teachers created one by selecting a specific

curriculum activity, such as finger painting on Wednesday. They struggled with the problem of selecting these special activities, because they did not want to artificially restrict the curriculum and subordinate the ongoing program to the requirements of a weekly calendar. One teacher decided to bring her guitar to school every Tuesday; this decision did not prohibit other kinds of music periods during the week. Other special curriculum activities included cooking special foods, such as a fruit dessert every Friday, and alternating the use of high-interest materials in the arts and crafts center, for example making play dough on Monday for use the rest of the week and finger-painting on Tuesday. This approach targeted special features of the ongoing curriculum for highlighting one day a week.

Another approach to recording important weekly events featured the management system for these events (Table 8.5). One teacher decided that, due to space constraints, all centers could not be accommodated every day, so she designated a closed center each day of the week, as illustrated in Table 8.6.

For each of these scheduling decisions, the calendar format of posting information provided the opportunity for children to answer their own questions about scheduled access to activities. Initially, the children's questions focused on that day's events, and subsequently they used the

Table 8.5
Weekly Schedule

Monday	Tuesday	Wednesday	Thursday	Friday	Saturday	Sunday
Picture of or samples of play dough materials: salt, flour, and food coloring	Picture of guitar or miniature guitar	Photograph of Mrs. Holmes, the special-projects art teacher	Picture of sneakers or miniature sneakers	Picture of different kinds of fruit and a cooking pot	Home Day	Home Day
Make play dough	Guitar	Mrs. Holmes, art teacher	Gymnasium	Cooking fruit	No school—2 days	

Table 8.6
Weekly Schedule: Interest Centers

Daily closing of one interest center to allow for a special activity. Other possibilities: special games or songs; special snacks; special cleanup of one center each day; special activity in a center each day.

Monday	Tuesday	Wednesday	Thursday	Friday	Saturday	Sunday
Literacy activity	Seasonal activity	Sand or sponge painting	Cooking activity	Dramatic activity with puppets and props	Home Day	Home Day
Easels closed	Woodworking bench closed	Sand table closed	Water table closed	Music listening center closed		

weekly calendar to anticipate the next day and the day after. We saw children gathered around the calendar strip, sorting out the information that it provided, as follows:

"Look. Yesterday we had music. Today is art."
"Yeah and then we're gonna have gym." "Yeah, tomorrow is gym."
"Look. Art. Gym, cooking, art. Gym, cooking, art."

When children spontaneously use the weekly calendar strip as a resource, a natural next step is to extend the use of a recording system to span more than one week.

A Multiple-Week Schedule of Events. The emerging curriculum of programs for four- and five-year-olds provides many opportunities to look at past and future events in terms of more than one week. Typical multiple-week activities which benefit from data recording include such science adventures as sprouting seeds and growing plants and observing the evaporation of water over a period of days. A sample list of curriculum activities that require planning ahead would include such perennial activities as class trips, classroom celebrations, and invited classroom guests.

Table 8.7 illustrates a two-week planning calendar devoted to planning for a trip. It could stand alone or be combined with the existing information on daily activities during a week. The value of retaining both pieces of information on the calendar is that children can ground the new schedule within a known schedule, using the known to bridge to the unknown. The disadvantage is the potential confusion that may result from multiple pieces of information located in one box.

Table 8.7 illustrates a two-week data-recording calendar. It can constitute a dedicated calendar, one that serves a specific purpose, since the information on other weekly activities is not useful in this task. Pictures and/or artifacts may be needed for children who are not yet reading standard script.

Personal Calendars. In kindergarten programs, where learning center activities are part of the daily program, personal calendars provide a powerful tool to involve children in planning and reviewing their own cur-

Table 8.7
Planning a Trip

Week 1

Monday	Tuesday	Wednesday	Thursday	Friday	Saturday	Sunday
		Visitor from farm	Read books about farm Send permission slips home	Read books about farm	Home Day	Home Day

Week 2

Monday	Tuesday	Wednesday	Thursday	Friday	Saturday	Sunday
Return permission slips Plan the farm trip	Review plans for farm trip Read more about the farm	Farm trip	Write thank-you letter to farm people	Mail thank-you letter to farm people	Home Day	Home Day

riculum engagements. Kindergarten teachers discovered that having children maintain their own daily recording of activities during center time set the context for increasing their thinking about their activities. It also provided the kind of record over time that children could review with a sense of pride. These diary-type calendars began with single-week formats. Children drew pictures or otherwise noted buildings they created with blocks, roles they took in the drama center, and books they listened to in the literacy center. Over a period of days, the teacher could talk with each child about his or her curriculum pursuit and encourage planning for further extensions of their ongoing activity in one center or exploration of another center. The record also served as a topic of conversation between children as they compared the information on the calendars. They were able to talk about their accomplishments; for example, "I built a firehouse." "Yeah, and I made a painting for my sister." "And look at this! I helped cook the applesauce we ate."

Because these calendars were cumulative records of children's involvement and accomplishments, teachers found that they were useful for communicating with parents at conference time. This expanded use of calendars fits well into the need for authentic assessment as a balance to standardized tests that was discussed in Chapter 6.

A Day-Date Calendar. The need to introduce number and month labels on calendars in preprimary programs may emerge when children express interest in locating their birthdays in a sequence of days and weeks. In kindergarten classrooms, as children gain expertise in using the calendar as a tool, it is likely that some will initiate a plan to enter a birthday on the calendar. At this stage of calendar usage, teachers will need to evolve the design that fits the level of understanding of the children in the group. Whether a birthday is entered on the weekly calendar strip or a birthday calendar is generated with more conventional organization of weeks in months depends upon the context. What is important is that the day–date calendar emerges in a way that fits children's developing mastery of written numbers, counting, reading, and the calendar as an important tool in their lives.

Using Calendars in Primary Classrooms

Once children have incorporated the use of the calendar into their way of thinking about planning and reviewing schedules and recording important information about activities in their school life, the possibilities

Table 8.8
Sprouting Seeds

Week 1

Monday	Tuesday	Wednesday	Thursday	Friday	Saturday	Sunday
Planted 10 lima bean seeds	0 sprouted	0 sprouted	1 sprouted	3 sprouted	Home Day	Home Day

Week 2

Monday	Tuesday	Wednesday	Thursday	Friday	Saturday	Sunday
7 sprouted	10 sprouted				Home Day	Home Day

for further use to support curriculum emerge with the ongoing program. The movement from child-constructed calendars to conventional adult calendars increases options for use.

In science, the calendar is a handy tool for planning of, and recording data on, experiments. Study of such topics as weather patterns associated with erosion, and plant cycles and seed sprouting, also benefit from data recording in a calendar format. (See Table 8.8 for a sample data recording of observations of seed sprouting.)

Clustering of months seasonally has meaning in these kinds of studies. Clustering of years into decades or centuries conforms with the use of timelines in order to help children to connect studies about long ago events and today's environment.

Using the Clock and Other Time-Recording Tools

Developing concepts of elapsed time during minutes and hours poses a greater challenge than during days and weeks. Adults as well as children perceive elapsed time in terms of their interest in the ongoing activity. One hour waiting for a highly anticipated event seems longer than one hour spent in an event of high interest. Once again, children learn best when the focus of the learning connects to their interests.

Everyday tools for recording minutes and hours that capture children's attention and can serve their interests within activities include three-minute-egg timers and kitchen timers. Less familiar tools that have great possibilities for supporting children's learning about time include sundials, hourglass timers, and pendulum timers. The time-measuring tool needs to fit the task if children are to increase their sense of elapsed time. Table 8.9 lists possibilities for meaningful use of the different minute and hour recording tools.

Table 8.9
Using Time-Recording Tools

Tool	Activity Possibilities	Mathematics Content
Analog clock	Information on regularly scheduled activities: e.g., lunch, arrival, departure, outdoor period, special events.	Matching configuration of "hands" on the clock; matching location of ends of "hands" coordinated with numbers on the clock face.
3-minute-egg timer	Pacing time on a short task, such as • "thinking up two words that . . ." • physical activities (dashing across the room) • one turn at a game	Estimating length of time that is needed to complete designated actions or tasks. Comparing durations of time. Developing realistic expectations for completing tasks and activities.
Hourglass (sand) timer	Scheduling program activities. Planning special events.	Developing realistic expectations for activities that require more than one hour.
Sundial	Investigating science events.	Coordinating relationship between sun and shadows and recording the movement of the sun by following change in orientation of shadow. Coordinating sundial information with analog clock information.
Pendulum timers	Measuring duration of brief science event, such as falling objects. Comparing time-recording tools.	Developing record-keeping system. Selecting the right tool for the task.

Concluding Remarks

The richness of curriculum offers many opportunities to use time-recording tools for data recording and analysis as well as for management and planning program. One context in which children need to be aware of time includes some of the games they play, discussed in Chapter 2. Chapters 9 and 10, dealing with curriculum links to science and social studies, suggest additional ideas for meaningful use of tools to measure time.

Note

1. This chapter is adapted from Schwartz, S. L. (1995), "Calendar Reading: A Tradition that Begs Remodeling," *Teaching Children Mathematics* 1 (2): 104–109. Reprinted with permission from *Teaching Children Mathematics,* © by the National Council of Teachers of Mathematics. All rights reserved.

References

Schwartz, S.L. (1995). "Calendar reading: A Tradition that begs remodeling." *Teaching Children Mathematics* 1 (2): 104–109.

Wann, K., Dorn, M., & Liddle, E. (1962). *Fostering intellectual development in young children.* New York: Teachers College Press.

CHAPTER 9

Science and Mathematics

Curriculum Partners

Young children are perpetually in the process of finding out "what happens when" and using their mathematical knowledge to describe what they are seeing. This chapter deals with how young children learn science concepts, provides examples of some concepts that they can learn, and discusses how mathematics provides many of the critical tools that are integral to science learning. Children use all their senses to collect information, and then they organize the information by comparing and contrasting it with prior understanding. This process of comparing and contrasting information involves mathematical thinking in the areas of number, geometry, and measurement.

> At the water table in the prekindergarten, three children were blowing onto the water using a straw.
> "Look at my circle. It's big."
> "Yeah, and mine is bigger. Look."
> They continue blowing, continuously commenting on the size of the circles they were creating.

These prekindergarten children are finding out about the effects of force on the surface of the water. They are using their knowledge of *shape* to talk about their discoveries.

> Two first-grade children sitting next to each other at a table waiting for the teacher to begin the next activity were comparing how far their pencils would roll when they flicked them with one finger.
> "Hey. It almost fell off, but it didn't."

In response, the second child declared: "Yeah, How did you do that? Mine rolled off."

These first graders are experimenting with movement of the pencils produced by physical force. Their understanding of the event involved thinking about *distance, direction,* and *location*.

In anticipation of a trip to a farm, the second-grade children were working with partners searching through books and magazines to find and list all the farm animals. One team became fascinated with pictures and text about mother–baby combinations. As if in unspoken agreement, they narrowed their search to mother–baby pairs, ignoring all other pictures of farm animals.

The attention of these children is on *pairing* mother and baby animals.

The Processes of Learning and Teaching Science

Some might argue that the investigative behavior illustrated above falls short of our definition of a professional scientist because the research is informal. However, there is no question that the children are using the scientific skills of inquiry outlined in the following list. Mathematics is an integral part of this process.

1. Initiating discovery

   Observing: using the senses—sight, taste, touch, hearing, and smell—to find out about objects and events in the environment

   Comparing: a newly perceived attribute, characteristic, or quantity with a known attribute or quantity, often involving measurement thinking

   Grouping and classifying objects and events according to their perceived characteristics

2. Extending discovery by repeated trials and preplanned experiments

   Collecting data: combining as many processes as necessary to obtain additional information about objects and events

   Communicating: conveying information by means of oral and/or written descriptions, demonstrations, pictures, graphs, and charts

3. Applying Knowledge

   Predicting: describing in advance the outcome of an event based on prior observations recorded verbally or in written form

4. Using Advanced Processes

Inferring: figuring out a conclusion that can only be mentally understood based on observations of an object or event

Interpreting data: explaining the meaning or significance of information regarding an object of event

Hypothesizing: arriving at general statements of concepts from observations and data

Experimenting by plan: designing and carrying out procedures to obtain reliable and more precise information about inter-relationships between and among objects and events.

The first step in investigating is *observing*, using the five senses to find out about objects and events, as the three-year-olds were doing at the water table. The processes of comparison and contrast constitute the core of all levels of inquiry. Children group like and unlike observations into collections or sets. Number, geometry, and measurement serve as tools to describe patterns of relationship within and between events and groups of objects. Each successive level of inquiry takes on more of the formal qualities of science research as children develop generalizations.

A critical part of the concept-building process occurs through communication with others about observations. Children initially communicate with gestures and oral language. As they mature children develop the ability to understand information in pictures and other forms of records that store information for review and analysis. Teachers who adapt science teaching to the different ways that children communicate about their understanding validate and extend the children's use of mathematics to collect and organize science information.

The Content of Scientific Learning and Teaching

Each field of science has a distinctive set of key concepts and related facts associated with the concepts. The adult who provides the materials and initiates interactions needs to be familiar with the key concept(s) connecting an unpredictable range of children's observations in order to support children's thinking about these observations. While it is not possible to become experts on all topics, teachers can review essential facts and concepts relative to planning a particular investigation.

The science knowledge base—the world of science content—is very large. Essentially, it includes physics and chemistry within the physical sciences; plant and animal life within the life sciences; and geology, astronomy, and weather and earth phenomena within the earth and environmental sciences. The body of scientific knowledge is changing so rapidly that it precludes the likelihood that any of us can achieve extensive fluency in all of the sciences (Martin 2003).

More than four decades ago, Jerome Bruner advanced the idea that "the foundations of any subject may be taught to anybody at any age in some form" (Bruner 1960). Therefore, adults need to understand the basic ideas governing the subject in order to provide opportunities for children to add to their knowledge at their level of understanding. This idea shifts the focus of teaching from transmitting facts to nurturing children's information collecting, organizing, and testing events for meaning.

The Connections between Content and Process

The content–process connections have been discussed several times in this book. The message is that there is no meaningful content without process and there is no process without content (Chalufour & Worth 2003; Harlen 1997; Harlen 2001; Martin 2003; Wasserman 1990). A noted science educator further elaborates on this interdependence between process and content: "[P]rocess skills cannot be used and developed independently of concepts and knowledge and, conversely . . . concepts and knowledge cannot be learned with understanding without the use of process skills" (Harlan 1993, p. 5). Mathematical tools serve both content and process goals.

As illustrated in the above vignettes, children constantly examine the properties of objects. After noticing an interesting event, they repeat it over and over to verify what has happened. Then, by accident or deliberation, they continue to expand their experiments to find out what happens when they try different actions with the objects. Initially, when observing events, children tune in to gross differences in measurement for which such terms as *bigger*, *more*, and *heavier* adequately communicate meanings for them. Through these experiences their understanding of relationships increases along with their desire to gain greater control over the use of the materials. At the same time, they extend their knowledge and discover more precise information as evidenced in their conversations with others.

Nurturing Science and Mathematics Learning

Teachers who nurture learning through inquiry increasingly focus questions on what information children are collecting, how to record and review it, and how to use it. For example, in the first vignette the children were experimenting with the physical laws of motion as they made circles on the surface of the water. The children's actions and conversation reveal that they are making connections between the blowing of air through a straw and the resulting effect on the surface of the water. The foundational ideas in physics related to this event are that (1) force produces change, (2) moving air is a force, and (3) some forces can be controlled, thereby controlling the change that occurs.

Armed with this knowledge, the adult can stimulate further exploration by beginning with a question that focuses on *how* the children are creating the circles. Once they explain what they are doing, the next level of stimulation could take the form of encouraging them to try to create different effects, such as making bigger or smaller circles or locating the circles at different positions on the surface of the water: "If you wanted to make your circles bigger, what would you do?" Their efforts to change size and/or location create a context for conversation about their actions and validate their thinking. In scientific terms, they are exploring the relationship between degree of force, direction of force, and result. The mathematical language of size and location, and perhaps speed, serve as tools to help children increase their understanding about the relationship between their actions and what is happening on the surface of the water.

The adult's follow-up questions are important after children succeed in changing the outcomes, because young children tend to accumulate a great many intuitive impressions. The adult's questions can help them organize their impressions and thereby refine the knowledge they have gained through manipulating the variable of moving air as a force.

Instructional Strategies

As we watch children actively forging their own learning, the perennial question is, "How do I further the learning of these children?" More often than not, our knowledge of content serves as the guide for selection from the options of both content and process. In addition to decisions on whether to *feed, lead,* or *seed,* and whether to validate or extend learning, as discussed in Chapter 6, instructional strategy decisions depend upon the science content.

Making Teaching Decisions to Nurture Inquiry

A colleague and I were present when the following classroom event occurred (Curcio & Schwartz 1997):

> Two kindergarten children were finding out what happens when they placed "counting bears" on the balance scale. One child put three bears on one scale plate and the other child put five on the other side. After observing the imbalance, the first child challenged his classmate, "Hey, what did you do? Wait. You have too many." He grabbed three and added them. The imbalance now shifted to the other side. At this point, the first child said: "No! You have too many." At this point they counted, matched the sets, and were satisfied. Next, they purposely changed the imbalance from one side to the other, declaring how many bears they had with each successive change.

When the two children had satisfied their curiosity about the way to use number to create balance and imbalance with the materials at hand, the time was ripe to focus on further weight comparisons. After validating through conversation what they discovered, we chose to *seed* the children's research efforts by adding large bears which were equivalent in weight to two small bears.

The Emergence of Algebraic Thinking

The two kindergarten children began to demonstrate algebraic thinking as they became fascinated with the proportional/ratio relationship in weight between two small bears and one large. My colleague posed the question, "Can you balance the scale with the mother bear on the tray by using the baby bears?" thereby provoking the initial discovery of the two-to-one relationship. After the children found that two baby bears make the scale balance with one mother bear, she posed the question of what would happen if another mother bear was placed in the scale pan. Through repeated problem-posing while increasing the number of mother bears, one child declared, "Oh. Now I know. I keep going up by twos." He identified the functional weight relationship of one-to-two, one mother to two babies.

In this interaction, my colleague chose to show the two children how this relationship might be recorded on paper using numerals:

1 mother = 2 babies

2 mothers = 4 babies

3 mothers = 6 babies

4 mothers = 8 babies

Another option would have been to ask the children to make their own record of what they discovered to share with their classmates or to use later to compare information collected when using different materials. It is likely they would have used the less sophisticated pictograph model, drawing pictures to represent their findings. This form of saving information constitutes the beginning of formalizing knowledge through data recording, a critical part of the science research process.

Mathematics Tools: Collecting and Recording Scientific Data

Graphing is one of the primary tools used to organize data in the sciences. (The term *graph* for early childhood, pre-K through grade 3, is used to refer to all forms of recorded information irrespective of the degree of organization of the data.)

Throughout history, data have been recorded in a variety of pictorial, graphic, and numeric formats. Cave records, rich with pictures and tallies, reveal how humans have historically kept records of important events. Today, media reports depend heavily on the use of graphs to present information and forward an interpretation of that information. A brief glance through many of the science education books reveals numerous recommendations for recording scientific phenomena as it occurs in nature as well as for recording the results of planned experiments. Recording options include tallies, charts, and sorted lists as well as standard bar graphs, line graphs, and circle graphs.

In Chapter 8, analysis of the complexity of adult calendars served as the rationale for examining ways to engage children in constructing calendars that related to their emerging concerns for organizing their time. The calendar, as they constructed it, served as a data recording instrument. An examination of adult forms of graphing in the section that follows reveals similar complexities.

Traditional graphing formats depend upon the ability to organize information mentally before recording it. Therefore, the decisions that precede the drawing of the graph include

- choosing the graphing format—bar graph, circle graph, line graph, tally; and
- labeling the parts of the graph to guide data entry—columns on a bar graph (X axis–Y axis), segments along the line connecting information on a line graph, grouping of tally marks, segments on a circle graph.

Both the persons graphing and the consumers of the graphed information need to be familiar with the dimensions of the topic under study in order to use it. Recall how many times it has been necessary to pore over a graph in the newspaper or magazine, trying to figure out what the Y-axis and the X-axis represent and the value of the units on the graph. These adult experiences remind us that much of what we consider "simple graphs" challenge the children in the same way graphs of less familiar content challenge us.

The National Council for Teachers of Mathematics has defined a sequence for developing competence in collecting, recording, and analyzing data that spans the schooling years from prekindergarten through grade 2. The four steps in the sequence are (1) formulating questions; (2) selecting and using appropriate statistical methods to analyze data; (3) developing and evaluating inferences and predictions that are based on data; and (4) understanding and applying basic concepts of probability (NCTM 2000). Meaningful engagement in each of these steps flows from helping children pose their own questions, choose their own ways to represent data, and then talk about what they have found out.

The Case for Child-Constructed Data Recordings

It is only recently that early childhood professionals have begun to explore ways to engage young children in recording data their own way rather than limiting instruction to the use of the adult model (Chalufour & Worth 2003; Schwartz 2004; Whitin 1997). In the past, recommendations for beginning experiences in graphing, irrespective of topic, usually featured the bar graph as the format of choice. The adult role was to provide the blank graph and show children how to use it.

The Limits of Copying "the Model." The conventional practice of showing children how to use a bar graph omits the process that data collectors go through as they record data prior to organizing it for better understanding. It ignores the reality that, before initiating the activity, the data collector must understand the relationship between the data that will be collected and the structure of the graph. Experienced producers of graphs also know how to create more than one format and can make selections based on an assessment of the most effective way to display the information.

Growing into Graphing. Children develop fluency in using graphs after they have collected information that interests them. They need experiences in successively moving through the stages of recording valued information. The ability to understand the information recorded on graphs requires that children experience collecting data in the following ways:

- They participate in selecting a topic of interest about which to collect information.
- They enter data as it is received and invent ways to represent the information.
- They interpret the recorded information and communicate with others.
- They reorganize the collected information to facilitate communication.

These experiences lead to the ability to plan more efficient formats or graph frames before collecting new information. Children's knowledge about different possibilities for graphing increases as they engage in successive experiences that summarize and interpret randomly recorded information and practice creating ways to make the information more accessible.

Young children may begin to collect and enter information by using objects to represent information. The preprimary child who represents information with a drawing may be the only one who understands the meaning of her drawing. When preprimary children enter information graphically, the meaning of the drawings to others depends upon the children's representational skills.

The Data-Collecting Process

Data collecting for curriculum purposes takes place in two different contexts, a group led by the adult and one in which children independently collect and record information.

Procedure for Developing Group Experiences in Graphing. Graphs developed by a whole group may deal with the collection of information relative to a daily activity or to science projects. For example, if the class is going to adopt a pet to take care of in school, one task is to list the survival needs of animals they are considering and assess the resources available to meet these needs. A list is one method of recording data.

The process begins when an adult or another child frames a question of interest to the children. As they collect information, it takes on meaning as children help devise a way to keep track of the information. When asked the question, "How are we going to remember this information?" we have found that children's suggestions are more varied than the bar graphs and written tallies that adults usually provide. Children's ideas more closely reflect the way they think about recording data. Children generated several ideas when brainstorming about recording information on the popular topic of weather, frequency of sunny days, rainy days, and windy days during one month:

- They drew a picture representing the weather at each corner of the recording sheet.
- They drew a miniature picture of the weather each day in the correct quadrant of a weather chart.
- They wrote about the weather each day on a list and then counted the days at the end of the month.
- They made a sorted list: they wrote the weather labels and then, each day, wrote the name of the day under the appropriate label.
- They used colored blocks—red meant a sunny day, etc.—and placed the block that stands for the weather in the collection box to be sorted at the end of the month.

Other familiar topics likely to evoke similar suggestions are keeping track of the growth of a plant over a period of time; creating a sorted list based on information gained from testing the power of magnets with a collection of objects, or experimenting with creating temporary magnets; and recording information about the number of seeds found in apples. More efficient formats emerge as children share their recorded information and discover better ways to organize for reporting.

Procedures for Developing Data Recording by Individuals. The other context for data recording is one in which children independently pursue the activity, collecting and recording information related to their own project or unique interests, such as recording the growth of seeds planted in an individual planter or conducting simultaneous experiments on water evaporation.

A current study devoted to "Explorations in Graphing with Prekindergarten Children" has revealed an unexpected range of mathematical understandings and skills (Schwartz 2004). The major insights gained from two years of developing graphing experiences with inner-city four-year-olds is that (1) when we give children opportunities to enter data their own way in high-interest contexts, they progressively refine their graphing skills toward more efficient and conventional formats, and (2) adults underestimate young children's capabilities for inventing ways to record information.

Science Activities that Integrate Mathematics

Choosing Topics and Instructional Strategies

Table 9.1 lists some of the traditional science activities in early childhood settings that offer opportunities to foster understandings in these fields of science along with the mathematics involved in the tasks.

Capitalizing on the Curriculum Possibilities

Teachers who plan to integrate science and mathematics activities first assess children's prior experiences in order to identify information that the children can collect during the experience.

Cooking Activities. Cooking activities integrate science, social studies, and mathematics. The rich well of possibilities for the selection of foods to serve on the holidays stems not only from the tradition of the holiday but also from the cultures of the children in the class.

The science concepts exposed in a cooking event provide opportunities for children to make connections between the forces of change and outcomes. The forces they can identify initially center on the direct physical acts of mixing, cutting, and molding, and expand to include such factors as temperature and chemical interactions.

Table 9.1
Science Content, Mathematics, and Related Activities

Science Area	Big Idea	Typical Activities Involving Mathematics
Physical Science Deals with physics and chemistry: Properties of objects Physical laws of motion Chemical laws of interaction	Objects have unique properties that distinguish them one from the other in terms of: Perceptual properties identified through the five senses Interaction with other materials identified through experimenting by combining through physical force, temperature changes, and chemical reactions Change properties identified through interaction and force	Experiments: Sinking and floating Absorbency, density Rolling and sliding Producing and responding to sounds Mixing fluids and solids Projects: Cooking Making plaster of paris molds Making finger paint and play dough
Life Science Deals with plant life and animal life	Understand that living things: grow and change reproduce vary in their rate of growth have unique attributes that distinguish them one from the other meet their needs for food and survival in different ways Living things vary in patterns of adaptation	Measuring growth over time: plants, animals, including humans comparing growth within and between plant and animal species

Table 9.1 (continued)

Science Area	Big Idea	Typical Activities Involving Mathematics
Earth and Environmental Science Deals with environmental materials and environmental events	The earth's surface is made up of a variety of materials.	Rock and soil comparisons.
	Weather phenomena affect all living things and objects in the environment	Direction and location of changes due to weather
	Water changes states	Temperature, time, and volume measures accompanying change in state of water
	Shadows are created when an object intersects a light source and a surface	Size measure, direction, and location of shadow, relation of light source to shadow

The mathematical measures used to describe changes in size, shape, and volume draw from number, geometry, and measurement.

In Table 9.2, the popular activity of making butter cookies illustrates a variety of opportunities for using mathematics to support the development of both science and mathematics understanding. As the activity is introduced, the first step of collecting and organizing the set of ingredients and tools required for the project activates a one-to-one matching task, as children compare the items on the list with the assembled materials, and check to assure that the set is complete. Serial ordering can be introduced by reviewing the recipe and placing the items into the order in which they will be used.

Making popcorn is another popular activity that is often underutilized for fostering science and mathematical thinking. The key science concept is that the properties of objects change when heat is applied. The information collected to support the emergence of this concept includes:

- The size of corn kernels increases when heated.
- Texture and color change.
- The number of kernels does not change.

Table 9.2
Making Cookies Integrates Mathematics and Science

Assembling and Organizing Ingredients and Tools

Mathematical relationships for discovery, practice, and problem solving	*Teacher inputs to support mathematical thinking and skills*	*Science Content*
One-to-one matching of the items.	"Let's check to make sure we have everything we need. List all ingredients and tools."	Form-function relationship: Anticipate the purpose of the tools and how they will be used:
Organizing the set of ingredients and the set of tools in order of use.	"Now let's line them up in the order we'll use them."	

Measuring and Mixing Ingredients

Mathematical relationships for discovery, practice, and problem solving	*Teacher inputs to support mathematical thinking and skills*	*Science Content*
Examining the meaning of *full-volume measures* and *partial-volume measures*. Practicing measuring volume. Associating whole number and fraction words with measured amounts.	"We measured one full cup of mix and it is here in this plate. Now for the sugar, we need to measure one half of a cup. Let's look at the difference in the amount of sugar and mix."	Unique properties of objects: Compare and contrast the properties of the cooking ingredients. Properties change when mixed (Note: save small amount of each material before mixing for comparison purposes.)

Forming the Cookies

Mathematical relationships for discovery, practice, and problem solving	*Teacher inputs to support mathematical thinking and skills*	*Science Content*
Making cookie shapes: Each person receives an equal amount of dough, enough to make a number of cookies. Children make cookies in different shapes, using plastic cutting utensils.	As variations in shapes begin to appear, focus attention on similarities and differences in attributes of shape and size. "Look at the different shapes you are making." Encourage children to compare, finding identi-	Creating standard and nonstandard geometric shapes. Matching identical and similar shapes. Comparing sizes of cookie shapes in terms of surface area and thickness. Comparing shapes,

Table 9.2 (continued)

Forming the Cookies (continued)

	cal, similar, and different shapes. Repeat the teaching strategy for comparing size and thicknesses. Repeat the teaching strategy for comparing combinations of shapes; example: gingerbread figure or building.	number of sides, rounded edges, and straight edges. Matching sides of different shapes.

Decorating the Cookies

Mathematical relationships for discovery, practice, and problem solving	*Teacher inputs to support mathematical thinking and skills*	*Science Content*
Decorating cookies with raisins, nuts, and dried fruit. Making patterns with materials added as decoration. Repeating patterns, varying patterns, and comparing patterns.	With an individual child, focus attention on the sequence or pattern being developed or change in pattern: "Let's look at the different ways you put the raisins (nuts, dried fruit) on the cookies." Invite children to describe and compare the "different ways of organizing the raisins, nuts; and dried fruit on the cookies." Look for repeated patterns and spatial order.	Physical properties of objects change when combined with other objects.

Cooking

Mathematical relationships for discovery, practice, and problem solving	*Teacher inputs to support mathematical thinking and skills*	*Science Content*
Spacing and pattern of placement of cookies on cookie sheet prior to cooking. Size and shape changes in cookies after cooking.	Draw attention to the spacing between cookies on a row and between rows before cooking. Draw attention to variations in shapes after cooking.	Heat changes the properties of objects, texture, size, shape, and color.

- A sound accompanies the change.
- There is a change in edible properties.

The information-collecting skills unify science and mathematical skills through observing changes that involve comparison in size, shape, and number.

Physical Science Activities. Physical science activities are equally engaging and involve extensive measurement and number possibilities. Whether they occur during child-directed activities in classroom interest centers or elsewhere, one major part of the teaching role is to capture teachable moments, as illustrated in the following vignette in which children were experimenting with structural balance:

> *The moment:* Two prekindergarten boys were building individual towers in the block area. The first boy declared, "Look, mine is taller." His classmate responded by placing more on top and stating, "No way. Mine is taller than yours." And then his building toppled.
>
> *Teaching by feeding the moment:* The teacher began building a structure next to the toppled structure and accompanied her activity by thinking aloud: "I wonder what would happen if I put more blocks on the bottom before I build it up."

Concluding Remarks

Mathematics provides critical tools integral to science learning. As children discover, experiment, and apply science understanding to their activities, they utilize number, geometry, measurement, and graphing to collect and organize their increasing body of knowledge. Similar connections between social studies and mathematics are discussed in the next chapter.

Recommended Reading

Chalufour, I., & Worth, K. The following three books are part of the the Young Scientist Series developed at the Educational Development Center, Inc., and published by Redleaf Press, St. Paul, MN. The books clearly define an approach to sustaining children's interest in discovering science based on a well-stated belief system and guides for developing activities in science. The activities feature data collecting and the use of number, geometry, and measurement to describe observations of objects and events: *Building struc-*

tures with young children (2004); *Discovering nature with young children* (2003); *Worms, shadows, and whirlpools* (2003).

Russell, H. (1973). *Ten-minute field trips: Using the school grounds for environmental studies*. Chicago: J.G. Ferguson Pub. Co. of Doubleday and Co.

References

Bruner, J. (1960). *The process of education*. Cambridge, MA: Harvard University Press.

Chalufour, I., & Worth K. (2003). *Discovering nature with young children*. St. Paul, MN: Redleaf Press.

Curcio, F. R., & Schwartz, S. L. (1997). "What does algebraic thinking look like and sound like with preprimary children?" *Teaching Children Mathematics* 3 (6): 296–300.

Folkson, S. (1996). "Exploring data: Kindergarten children do it their way." *Teaching Children Mathematics* 2 (6): 382–386.

Forman, G., & Kuschner, D. (1983). *The child's construction of knowledge: Piaget for teaching children*. Washington, DC: National Association for the Education of Young Children.

Harlen, W. (1993). *Teaching and learning primary science*. 2nd ed. London: Paul Chapman Publishing.

———. (2001). *Primary science: Taking the plunge*. 2nd ed. Portsmouth, NH: Heinemann.

Kamii, C., & DeVries, R. (1993). *Physical knowledge in preschool education: Implications of Piaget's theory*. New York: Teachers College Press.

Martin, D. (2003). *Elementary science methods: A constructivist approach*. 3rd ed. Belmont, CA: Wadsworth Thomson Learning.

National Council of Teachers of Mathematics (NCTM). (2000). *Principles and standards for school mathematics: Data analysis and probability*. Reston, VA: NCTM.

Schwartz, S. L. (2004). "Explorations in graphing with prekindergarten children." In Clarke, B., Clark, D., et al. *International perspectives on learning and teaching mathematics*, pp. 83–97. Goteborg, Sweden: National Center for Mathematics Education.

Wasserman, Selma. (1990). *Serious players in the primary classroom*. New York: Teachers College Press.

Whitin, D. (1997). "Collecting data with young children." *Young Children* (Jan. 1997): 28–32.

Worth, K., & Grollman, S. (2003). *Worms, shadows, and whirlpools*. Portsmouth, NH: Heinemann; Newton, MA: EDC; Washington, DC: NAEYC.

CHAPTER 10

Social Studies and Mathematics

Curriculum Partners

The social studies curriculum for preprimary and primary grades typically focuses on a wide range of topics reflecting a broad scope of social science disciplines. *Sociology*, the "systematic study of the development, structure, interaction and collective behavior of organized groups of human beings" (*Webster's Collegiate Dictionary* 1993), probably heads the list for source of topics in the early childhood years. From sociology flows the emphasis on self-knowing, self-valuing, and group membership. *Anthropology* also contributes to the multicultural focus. In addition, *geography, history, government, and politics* are often viewed as distinct subject areas, although it can be argued that government and politics as well as history and geography are integral dimensions of understanding current culture and the role of its members. In each of these fields, mathematics serves as a major tool in collecting, recording, and organizing information. In turn, students can use information to analyze events which can lead in turn to generalizations.

The Social Studies Content

The National Council for the Social Studies defines social studies as "the integrated study of the social sciences and humanities to promote civic competence." It is not a singular field, but rather a discipline that draws from many diverse disciplines, including anthropology, archaeology, economics; geography, history, philosophy; political science, psychology, religion; sociology, humanities, mathematics; and the natural sciences (Seefeldt & Galper 2000, p. 40).

Given the diverse fields that shape the social studies curriculum, it is no surprise that educators differ in their views of what and how to teach in this comprehensive curriculum. Some early childhood teachers take a child-centered approach to social studies that emphasizes social development, while other teachers stress more of a society-centered approach that focuses on citizenship and democratic principles. A third common approach, centering on the attainment of knowledge, includes ways of knowing and focuses on key concepts from the various social science disciplines (Jantz & Seefeldt 1999; Schwartz & Robison 1982).

When thinking about the academic fields listed above, it is possible to envision charts, tables, and graphs that explain the ideas to shape topics and support the "ways of knowing" approach to teaching. This is an approach that focuses on teaching children the skills of collecting, recording, organizing, interpreting, and reporting information as part of an essential, active process designed to develop understanding of the social studies. Thus, understanding social studies topics requires not only the acquisition of conventional knowledge but also an understanding of the tools that are used to collect and translate information for communication.

The Mathematics Content in Social Studies

The process of collecting and recording data offers one of the richest contexts for developing mathematical graphing skills in order to make sense out of the vast amount of societal information. Fluency with how to collect, record, and analyze information provides the foundation for the acquisition of knowledge in the social sciences. Graphing involves a full range of mathematical skills and understanding in sets, number, shape and space geometry, and measurement.

Collecting Data in Social Studies

The design of data-collecting experiences for use in the social studies curriculum follows the same basic instructional approach discussed in the previous chapter. The process begins with framing of a question that is of genuine interest to children. Next, children participate in devising the way to collect and record the information. Finally, they summarize, analyze, interpret, and use the recordings.

Young children can use group graphs when there is a recurring need to collect information by the group in order to make class decisions. These decisions typically deal with curriculum projects, celebrations, trips, fairs, and presentations. A listing of children's ideas and opinions launches the process, and subsequent lists of resources and needs guide further planning and serve as a reference for decisions and review. Individual graphs are useful for activities that are pursued by individuals and are driven by individual interests. Surveys are typical of this approach.

Whether recorded by the group or an individual, the data-collecting experience simultaneously serves two curriculum areas. In social studies, it provides public access to recorded information, available for referral as needed, and it leads to the framing of additional questions that have not yet been answered. In mathematics, the summary of collected information takes form through the use of graphic, numeric, and alphabetic entries available for analysis; the reorganization of the data; and the identification of further information needs.

The Developmental Sequence for Data Collection and Representation

The least sophisticated form of data entry identified in our work with very young children is placement of drawings in random order to represent the responses to a survey question (Schwartz 2004). No sorting or grouping occurs at this beginning level. The follow-up experience of sharing the collected information stimulates the development of more sophisticated organization of the recorded information, making it more easily accessible for summarizing, analyzing, and communicating to others.

The developmental pattern of representations follows a sequence from pictorial, to graphic, and finally to alphabetic and symbolic entries. The organization of the entries progresses from (a) random, to (b) clustering, to (c) lining up horizontally, vertically, or in circular array, to (d) tallies, and then to (e) bar graphs with one or two of the axes marked.

The Social Studies Curriculum in Action

Over the last decade, local as well as national curriculum publications have addressed common foci of the Social Studies Curriculum for the kindergarten and primary grades. The curricular designs feature goals within both the child-centered and society-centered approaches:

- self-knowing: developing awareness of self as a growing individual;

- self-valuing: demonstrating a growing knowledge about and appreciation of self, as well as the diversity of others in their communities; and

- group membership: realizing that (in the United States) most people live in families or family-like groups, and most children spend large amounts of time in school groups; groups fulfill different functions and have rules, defining roles and expectations, for fulfilling the functions; each individual has a role as a member of a family, school, and larger community; and group membership changes and group functioning evolves in relation to changing membership and setting.

As we entered the twenty-first century, the momentum of the public demand for more precision on curriculum content propelled an increase in the above list to include the familiar subject areas and to embrace prekindergarten as well. For example, the 2003 edition of prekindergarten performance standards in New York City added the following key social studies concepts to their list:

- *history:* understanding that change and continuity relate past events to their present and future events;

- *geography:* develop a growing understanding of position in space, geographic location, and direction;

- *sociology:* recognize the contributions of community workers as they produce goods or provide services; and

- *life science:* understand that all people have basic needs.

Historically, early childhood program practices for prekindergarten and kindergarten have been shaped by the child-centered and society-centered approach, whereas the practices at the primary grade level have tended to focus on citizenship and topics associated with sociology. At both levels, curriculum activities begin when teachers first facilitate children's adjustment to a new school group; as the year progresses, activities then include attention to the seasonal and holiday crafts and also include popular social studies projects. The following sections outline the ways in which mathematics serves the pursuit of activities.

Integrating Mathematics and Social Studies

An Example of Facilitating Adjustment to a New School Group. A large number of traditional activities during the early weeks of school target children's adjustment to the new school group. Curriculum activities focus on the above identified goals of self-knowing, self-valuing, and group membership. Irrespective of teacher commitments to the developmental, citizenship, or key-ideas perspectives, instructional decisions typically focus on ways to support children's adaptation to the classroom community. Teachers begin by collecting and organizing information about the members of the class and then publishing this information at the children's level of understanding. The data collection takes the form of lists, charts, and graphs.

In preprimary groups the focus is on helping children recognize their own name and then the names of the other children in the group. In most primary classrooms, children are already familiar with their own names. The ritual for getting to know classmates quickly shifts from introductions to sharing personal information about self and family.

An Example of Name Recognition in a Preprimary Group. In the following vignette, pattern and number feed the activity.

> It is the first week of school. The kindergarten children are gathered on a rug in a meeting area to begin the day. The teacher is silently clapping out sound patterns, one at a time, and the children are figuring out whose name the pattern might fit. *Clap. Clap, Clap.* Pause. *Clap, Clap, Clap.* The children begin to simultaneously call out different names, *A-mal-ya. El-i-ot, Fer-nan-do*, chanting in rhythm with the teacher's clapping pattern. When no more names are forthcoming, the teacher stops clapping. She recalls the names she heard, asking for verification from the children, and then, with the children, vocalizes each name, testing it against the pattern. When a name does not fit the pattern, she claps the pattern that does fit the name.

The mathematical skill is that of matching item for item between sets, one syllable of a name to one clap. From the social studies lens, the teacher is building a sense of community as children gain increasing familiarity with the names of their classmates. From the literacy perspective, the activity supports phonemic awareness, the sound structure of words.

An Example of Writing Names. Familiarity with the representation of one's name using alphabet letters involves recognition of several factors, specifically the number, shape, and sequence of letters. Involving children in charting their names in graph form highlights the number of letters in a defined measurement context. Participation of the children in the experience is critical to helping them understand how the graph reveals information. If the chart is made by the adult and presented to the children, they do not have access to the thinking involved in organizing the information; they only see the product. If children have a role in the production of the graph by recording the information and helping enter information, the product is in no small measure theirs because the information came from them and was recorded by them. They can, and will, return to the graph to extend their ownership of its contents.

An Example of Using Literature to Launch an Integrated Curriculum Activity. One example of this integrated approach to a set of curriculum activities for kindergarten or first-grade children, from a literacy program developed by me and by others, combines name graphing—mathematics—with a literature—literacy—experience in order to strengthen children's sense of community—social studies (Shilling & Schwartz unpublished). The story line in the book *Chrysanthemum* (Henkes 1991) centers on the early days of kindergarten. The main character is subject to teasing from her kindergarten peers for having such a long name and one that is really a name of a flower. As the story line develops, the children's views change through interactions with a well-liked music teacher who shares with the children her love of the name Chrysanthemum and thinks about other flower names for her unborn child. In response to the music teacher's invitation to think about possibilities, the children start generating lists of names of flowers, and, in the process, begin comparing the length of the names of flowers with their own names. The story line clearly targets the development of a sense of community based on valuing all members.

One of the follow-up plans in the curriculum unit features the use of children's names as the beginning experience of using graphs in order to discover additional information about their names. The following sequence for engaging young children in constructing a name graph was field-tested in over 100 classrooms with considerable success in stimulating children's interest in graphing data using a model:

1. Show a prepared name strip of Chrysanthemum and invite the children to verify the number of letters, as declared in the story.

2. Using their own name cards, ask children to find out the number of letters in their own name. Share information and propose a class name graph.

Figure 10.1.

3. Distribute one blank graphing strip to each child (see Figure 10.1). If necessary, remind children to place only one letter in each box.

   The guidelines for sequencing shape the instructional decision about how children will enter the letters of their name on the strip. The plan rests on the teacher accurately assessing the children's levels of skill from copying to creating. The simplest form for replicating a name is using preprinted letters to assemble the name while using the name card as the information source. The next level is to replicate from memory while using the preprinted letter cards without the name card as a prop. The level of difficulty increases when using letter stamps followed by the use of a writing tool. Again, the use of the name card as a guide precedes writing the name from memory.

4. Once the strips are completed, place them on a master name graph (see Figure 10.2).

5. The graph now offers many opportunities for children to uncover relationships, by comparing and contrasting the number of letters

C	h	r	y	s	a	n	t	h	e	m	u	m
J	o	r	g	e								
A	m	a	l	y	a							
C	h	r	i	s	t	o	p	h	e	r		
S	a	m	u	e	l							
E	l	i	a	s								
S	o	p	h	i	e							

Figure 10.2.

in the sets that represent the names and by analyzing the chart in other ways that might interest them.

The ways in which children analyzed this graphed information varied. In one class, the children's independent examination of the chart sparked a search to find out which letter appeared most often and least often. In another group, the teacher fed their interest by helping the children create an alphabet chart and then graphing how many times each letter appeared on the name chart. The meanings of "none" and the "empty set" captured their attention as they discovered that some alphabet letters were not on the chart. The discovery provoked an environmental print search, during which children developed their own recording strategies and ultimately converted their accumulated data to a traditional bar graph.

It was fascinating for adults to discover how quickly children will use a mathematical tool when it furthers their interest in finding out, as in this case. Note that the potential for generating ideas about probability also occurs as children get interested in looking at the frequency of letters on the graph. The question can then arise as to whether the letter distribution discovered on the name chart and in environmental print will be the same if one were to look at the text of one page in a favorite book.

An Example of Integrating Personal Information as Data. In a similar fashion, the collecting and recording of data about the personal information of the members of the class group conforms with the child-centered approach featuring self-valuing and group membership. In my work with prekindergarten children, many four-year olds evidenced strong interest in finding out about the likes and dislikes, families, and activity choices of their peers (Schwartz 2004). Following the initial collection of the information, the four-year-olds were able to report what they found out by using a variety of levels of number sense. In the less sophisticated summaries, children relied on general quantitative terms such as *some, a lot, nobody (not any)*, whereas the more mathematically developed children used number words to report what they found out. What we learned from this experience is that adults tend to underestimate children's potential to generate formats to record and interpret information that interests them.

A book that can be used to spark inquiry about peers is *We Are All Alike, We Are All Different* (Cheltenham Elementary School Kindergarteners 1991). The purpose of the book, stated on the back cover, is to reinforce "multicultural and anti-bias learning and appreciation." The brief text, with accompanying illustrations by the children, addresses those topics that typically enter into kindergarten children's conversations—their physical attributes, family makeup, homes, and likes and dislikes. The first set of characteristics in the book center on face and hair—eye color, hair color, hair length, and hair texture. The decision about whether to collect and record this information with the whole class group using a prepared graph format or to follow up with surveys by individual children depends upon the group context. If the adult chooses to pursue the activity with the total group after reading the book, a recording form might take the form of a simple unsorted list of hair color, followed by other attributes, each on separate sheets of paper. The selection of attributes flows from the children and the recordings reflect their suggestions of how to represent the responses. A summary of the findings may well lead to a need to better organize the information. Table 10.1 evolved with one group of children.[1] The data can subsequently be analyzed at several levels, from simply noting which names appear in each category to comparing quantities.

An Example of Integrating Body Measurement. A popular activity in early childhood programs is measuring the height of all members of the class group and entering this information on a chart placed on a classroom wall. A typical chart depicted in Figure 10.3 shows a measuring stick placed vertically using the floor as the baseline. Each child's name appears on a horizontal line along the measuring stick, indicating height. In order to understand this chart, the child needs to transform the meaning of the horizontal line with the name on it to a vertical line that begins at the name line and goes to the floor. In fact, the line with the name does

Table 10.1
Data Chart for Recording
Information about Hair

Length	Color	Type
Long	*Black*	*Curly*
(name)	(name)	(name)
(name)	(name)	(name)
Medium	*Brown*	*Straight*
(name)	(name)	(name)
(name)	(name)	(name)
Short	*Blonde*	*Nappy*
(name)	(name)	(name)
(name)	(name)	(name)

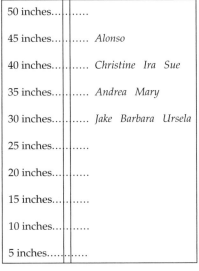

50 inches...	.....
45 inches...	..... *Alonso*
40 inches...	..... *Christine Ira Sue*
35 inches...	..... *Andrea Mary*
30 inches...	..... *Jake Barbara Ursela*
25 inches...	.....
20 inches...	.....
15 inches...	.....
10 inches...	.....
5 inches...	.....

Floor

Figure 10.3.

not represent the height of the child but rather where the body ends at the top of the head. The actual height of the child is represented by an *unseen* line that connects the name line with the floor. In this kind of height chart, you cannot see the line, only imagine it. Interviews with many prekindergarten and kindergarten children reveal that, although they can locate their own name, many cannot explain the relationship between the name line and their height. They will explain, "That's me," as they point to where their name is written.

From a mathematical perspective, a more concrete representation of height requires a strip of cardboard, rope, or yarn that is congruent with the height of the child.

It is also important to note that because of the common pattern of adult–child conversations that link growing taller with the highly touted value of "growing up," this activity may unleash a competitive and ego-threatening climate based on the notion that "taller is better." This activity, combined with ones that focus on other physical attributes, creates an opportunity to reinforce valuing the uniqueness of each individual.

Surveys That Integrate Social Studies and Mathematics. The multicultural curriculum centers on acquiring knowledge about, and respect for, similarities and differences between individuals, families, and cultural groups. The use of graphs to enhance self-knowing and self-valuing discussed earlier in this chapter is further extended through surveys in which children take the main role. As noted in the *Anti-Bias Curriculum* (Derman-Sparks 1989), there is research documentation for the idea that, "children begin to notice differences and construct classificatory and evaluative categories very early" (p. 1). Additionally, "societal stereotyping and bias influence children's self-concept and attitudes toward others." In this social context, one method for advancing multicultural understandings is to use surveys developed and completed by the children and then discussed in groups.

Attributes of culture are the objects used in daily life, such as clothing, food, jewelry and body decorations, music, and literature, reflected in the way people conduct their lives. Some cultural attributes are language, salutations and greetings; holidays and celebrations; ceremonies and rituals; customs; ways of observing rules and regulations; eye contact; physical and spatial contact (e.g., touch); traditions; and relationship within families.

The multicultural segment of the social studies curriculum features knowledge about, and respect for, attributes of diverse cultures as well as individual differences within cultural groups (Derman-Sparks 1989; Williams & DeGaetano 1985). For young children, the knowledge begins when they identify similarities and differences in others within their own immediate environment.

Getting Started with Surveys: A Review. The critical steps in initiating a survey activity are:

1. Framing the Question for Surveys. The initial experiences need to flow from questions children have generated for themselves. Irrespective of grade level, the topic for survey experiences selected by young children inevitably begins with those questions that help them define themselves in relation to others, such as what they like, what they wear, with whom they live, pets, favorites foods, and favorite activities (Schwartz 2004; Taylor 1997; Whitin 1997).

2. Providing the Tools and Nurturing the Process of Creating the Recording Format. Clipboards or tablets with unlined paper offer a relatively easy way to handle the process of collecting and recording responses to questions. The blank paper allows children to enter data their own way, with pictures, nonmathematical symbols, or numbers.

3. Collecting and Summarizing Survey Findings. The organization of this information follows the sequence of the initial collection of data.

4. Analyzing and Interpreting the Findings. The main purpose of collecting information is to obtain knowledge. Communication through discussion draws on interpretation of information collected and often leads to a need for further information.

Seasonal Crafts Integrate Social Studies and Mathematics

A focus on developing knowledge of different cultures and respect for their values and living patterns presents multiple opportunities to use mathematics to support the curriculum. One popular set of curriculum activities surrounds the holidays.

Every season and holiday poses challenges for teachers as they select and implement craft activities.[2] Many of these activities, such as holiday crafts, appear so regularly that they are considered part of the schooling tradition. When children produce those crafts that are the artifacts of cultural holidays celebrated nationally, or within the individual communities, the use of mathematical skills and understandings is integral to the process. Once again, instructional decisions about how to promote children's use of mathematical thinking in any given project evolves from our map of the content, the sequence of the process of learning, and our knowledge of what understanding and skills the children bring to the task.

Craft Projects

The image of preprimary and primary children leaving school at times of seasonal changes and major holidays most always includes craft or art projects clutched in their hands. In response to this perceived need to produce a craft for every holiday and change of season, the publishing community offers books dedicated to the subject. The detailed, step-by-step instructions on how to produce each craft beckon to teachers, encouraging them to use these books as manuals. However, providing children with models to copy delegates craft activities to an assembly-line approach that is missing not only the social studies content about cultural traditions but also rich opportunities to foster the use of mathematical skills and understanding in meaningful contexts. Craft activities depend so much on mathematical understandings and skills that they beg to be featured in authentic and meaningful ways.

When we focus the approach to the crafts on contributing to children's understanding of the context and use of the craft product, whole-class craft productions give way to individualized products that evolve from children's experiences and more accurately reflect individual children's design and construction abilities. From this vantage point, we turn our attention to one of the mathematics standards: "to build on the wholeness of their (the children's) perspective of the world and expand it to include more of the world of mathematics" (NCTM Standards 1989).

Process-Product Relationships

Production standards almost always pose a dilemma. If we value the process of developing the skills and understanding that craft activities evoke, then, by adult standards, the products are likely to be unfinished. If we place greater value on the product over the process, then we deny children the right to create and design, to learn through their own efforts, and to set their own standards.

Contrary to conventional wisdom, teaching plans which focus on children's thinking during the process of making a craft product need not abandon a concern for the quality of the product. Rather, such an emphasis on the decisions that are made along the production route provides an important context for children to evaluate the product and secure some understandings of process-product relationships. For example, when a child who is creating a decorative placemat for a special event varies the length of the opposite edging strips, the teacher has an opportunity to initiate a conversation with the child, comparing the effects of using noncongruent, or unequal, length strips and experimenting with possibilities (see Figure 10.4).

If the teacher wants to strengthen the measurement thinking that seems to be occurring, then some dialogue between teacher and child is needed at two points in the process: first, at the point where it becomes evident that the child is creating a noncongruent edging pattern and next, when the product is complete and the child is surveying the results. The initial dialogue can take the form of a teacher observation, "Oh, I see you are making this side edge strip shorter than the other side edge" (validating the child's actions) or an inquiry, "Are you planning to make more side strips at different lengths like these?" (extending the child's actions). This teacher talk assures that the child's measurement thinking will move from the intuitive to the conscious level.

The follow-up dialogue at the end of the task then can refer back to this midway conversation, focusing on the outcome: "You made these

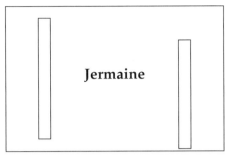

Figure 10.4. Placemat Decorated with Two Unequal-Length Strips

side strips different lengths. Did it turn out the way you wanted/expected it to look?" (reflecting on the child's actions).

The dilemma about process–product values resolves itself through the adult's instructional interactions during the process. This sharing of ideas and thoughts, sometimes referred to as *oral rehearsal*, not only helps the child to understand his or her own reasoning, but provides insight into conflicting and complementary perspectives (Dunn & Larson 1990). Further, it enhances the children's ability to use mathematical thinking to control outcomes and to set their own standards.

Criteria for Designing Craft Activities

Several criteria guide decisions about what learning to target as children engage in mathematical thinking and problem solving as they engage in craft experiences. Essentially, mathematical thinking occurs under one of two conditions: (1) when discovering a relationship, an initial learning, or (2) when applying their understanding of a relationship to a task, an application. Many experiences support children's growth from the discovery of a relationship in number, geometry, and measurement to the internalization of an understanding.

Discovery of Mathematical Relationships. When a young child manipulates materials and discovers relationships, we do not always have access to the child's thinking at this discovery point unless the youngster spontaneously talks as he thinks. The natural teaching inclination is to ask questions. However, with very young children this can be problematic for two reasons. First, catching the right moment is tricky. Asking the questions too soon interrupts thinking in progress. If we wait too long, the child has moved on to another concern, and the question fails to have relevance. Second, the child may not be able to express intuitive under-standings. Since observing and interviewing children about their mathe-matical strategies during independent discovery activities offers the only access time, we must continue to probe, but with caution.

Application of Mathematical Understandings of Relationships. Probably the most significant mathematical thinking occurs during an application ex-perience because children are selecting a mathematical route to a goal. If the route fails to achieve the goal, children are provoked to reexamine their un-derstandings. Under these circumstances, the point of access for teaching is much more direct. The most difficult challenge for the adult is finding ways to extend children's thinking about mathematical relationships without lead-ing them or doing their thinking for them by providing solutions.

Repeated Use of Mathematical Skills in Craft Activities. Some activ-ities can be designed to feature children's repeated use of a skill, such as pasting one geometric form in each box of a class-produced lotto board. Such activities, although important in fostering necessary skill mastery— in this case, discrimination of standard geometric forms—offer the least opportunity for either discovery or application of understandings of mathematical relationships. If, on the other hand, children were directed to make sure that no adjoining shapes were the same, or that there were no duplicate shapes on a line, practice and problem solving converge.

Integrating Mathematics with Craft Activities

The most meaningful learning occurs when children build on their rep-ertoire of understanding and skills toward ends that they care about. The decision on how to organize a craft project grows out of our knowledge of the children's prior experience with the materials. If children are es-sentially unfamiliar with the materials, the context for using the materials needs to feature *finding out* or *discovering*. On the other hand, if the chil-dren are familiar with the properties of the materials and have had ex-perience manipulating those properties, the context for use changes from *finding out* to *figuring out*, or from *discovery* to *application*. The frame for each of these two approaches is distinctively different.

The Finding-Out Model: Children Discover Mathematical Relationships

In the finding-out model, the children have opportunities to use un-familiar materials that help them to find out the mathematical relationships within the materials. Because the materials are unfamiliar, the final product emerges rather than follows a preset plan. In the following example, the context is the Halloween season. In this community, the holiday celebrations take many forms. The first-grade teacher has chosen to deal with the pervasive excitement driven by forces outside the classroom by planning with the children an in-class Halloween celebration without costumes. Following read-aloud stories about the history of Halloween and discussions about the different traditions for celebrating the holiday the teacher proposes an in-class celebration for which children will create *artifacts,* props to use during the celebration. For materials, the teacher provides a collection of small, variously-sized cardboard boxes and sheets of cardboard that the children have never used before in craft projects.

Teachers and children have had prior experience discussing their earlier extensive work with diverse materials in collage collections, including the construction of three-dimensional collages, mobiles, and decorative tabletop items, as well as daily block-building experiences in which they have discussed the size, shape, and purpose of structures.

The task is to create a craft product that they can use at the class Halloween party. The possibilities that children might generate include a "goblin" house, a centerpiece for the table, a mobile, or a storage container for the Halloween cookies.

Those mathematical discoveries that are most likely to occur involve measurement and geometry:

1. Some sides and surfaces match while others do not.
2. One large box may be attached on one side to two smaller boxes.
3. All rectangular boxes have the same number of sides/surfaces.
4. The height of the chain of boxes affects how well it "stands up."
5. A horizontal chain of boxes with the same number of items looks different than a vertical chain.
6. The same number of connected boxes does not always produce the same length of boxes.

If some styrofoam or other rounded materials are included in the collection, additional discoveries would revolve about the relationship between curved and straight edges. For example, curved edges do not have sufficient surface area to attach easily to straight edges.

Listening to children's conversations frequently reveals information which is not necessarily visible. When adults sit near the action as observers, some children invariably include them and share their discoveries, offering opportunities for the adults to validate and extend the children's reasoning.

The Figuring-Out Model: Children Apply Mathematical Knowledge

In the figuring-out model, just the reverse situation is created: the product is identified instead of the materials, and the child chooses the materials and the process instead of the product. This kind of activity presupposes that the children have had considerable experience with the materials from which they will choose to make the craft project. Therefore, they can plan the task and will engage in solving various mathematical problems which arise as they work at completing their plan. In this example, the context is that each child has designed and created a present to take home as a "Parent-day" gift. The products vary, representing individual decisions about what to make and how to make it, and the final step in this project is to wrap the gifts. The task is for the children to cut and decorate material for wrapping "Parent-day" gifts the children have already completed.

Children have had prior experience decorating paper and cardboard with graphic and collage materials, working with fabric and yarn, and stringing assorted materials.

For materials, the classroom contains various kinds of paper, graphic and plastic materials, collage collections, fabric, yarn and rope collections, and variously-sized cardboard containers which children may use.

One major set of mathematical challenges embedded in this task involves linear and weight measurement. Children need to measure and compare the size of the wrapping paper with the item to be wrapped, and they need to consider the strength of the wrapping paper in terms of the weight of the item. In addition, children will create their own mathematical challenges within the decorative design process.

Mathematics and Media Projects

Multiple possibilities emerge for integrating the mathematics curriculum with the media projects in the social studies curriculum. Table 10.2 illustrates the variety of ways to feature mathematics as children pursue the arts and crafts components of the social studies topics. However, in order to capitalize on these possibilities through instructional interac-

Table 10.2
Integrating Mathematics with Seasonal and Holiday Crafts

Season or Holiday	Materials	Mathematical Skills and Understanding
Autumn in temperate climates	Pine cones: stringing, constructing sculptures, mobiles.	Comparison of size and shape of cone and cone parts; comparison of weight of completed sculptures, mobiles
Halloween	Pumpkin seeds: seed collage, glued on as decorative coating for a bottle or can	Comparison of size, weight, number in the craft projects
Thanksgiving	Use of dried corn kernels to make collages or jewelry or to decorate containers and mobile items	Comparison of size, weight, number under varying conditions Identification and comparison of standard and nonstandard geometric shapes created on collages
December holidays	Model artifacts' use in the family home celebrations	Solving construction problems: matching lengths or sides of geometric shapes, size comparisons, creation of new shapes by joining nonidentical shapes (i.e., a square and triangle) to create a house with a slant roof Full range of mathematics ideas and content in number, geometry and measurement, and patterning for 4- and 5-year-olds Estimating sizes and amounts
Valentine's Day	Creating collages and patterns with hearts, diamonds, and other familiar environmental shapes	Discovering relationship between nonstandard shapes Comparing number of items in product and size of products

tions, it is necessary to anticipate the mathematical relationships and important ideas with which children will be dealing.

Concluding Remarks

In summary, pursuit of the wide range of social studies topics involves mathematical thinking and skills as an integral part of the activities. One aspect of social studies for young children, "citizenship education," or responsibility within a group and autonomy in decision making, is discussed in the next chapter.

Notes

1. The Child's World unit in the CUNY Literacy Enhancement Project includes additional ideas for using charts and graphs to support *self-knowing* and *self-valuing* activities initiated through literature.

2. This section is adapted from Schwartz, S. L. (1994), "Seasonal crafts: Discovering mathematical relationships and solving mathematical problems," *Teaching Children Mathematics* 1 (4): 214–219. Reprinted with permission from *Teaching Children Mathematics*, © by the National Council of Teachers of Mathematics. All rights reserved.

Recommended Reading

Dacey, L. S., & Eston, R. (1999). *Growing mathematical ideas in kindergarten*. Sausalito, CA: Math Solutions Publications. Provides vivid descriptions via a teacher's voice of activities to bring mathematics to life in a kindergarten class.

Folkson, S. (1996). "Meaningful communication among children: Data collection." In Elliott, P., & Kenney, M. (Eds.), *Communication in mathematics*, pp. 29–35. National Council of Teachers of Mathematics 1996 Yearbook. Reston, VA: NCTM. A narrative report of one kindergarten teacher's implementation of data-collecting activities including her insights developed through the experiences.

Whitin, D., Mills, H., & O'Keefe, T. (1990). *Living and learning mathematics*. Portsmouth, NH: Heinemann. Chapter 5 describes a variety of ways to integrate graphs into the curriculum. Topics include "exploring personal surveys," "constructing graphs to make classroom decisions," and "using graphs to learn." Samples of children's work illustrate the ideas.

References

Cheltenham Elementary School Kindergartners. (1991). *We are all alike. We are all different*. New York: Scholastic.

Derman-Sparks, L., & A.B.C. Task Force. (1989). *Anti-bias curriculum: Tools for empowering young children*. Washington, DC: National Association for the Education of Young Children.

Dunn, S., & Larson, R. (1990). *Design technology—children's engineering*. New York: Falmer Press.

Henkes, K. (1991). *Chrysanthemum*. New York: Greenwillow Books.

Jantz, R., & Seefeldt, C. (1999). "Early childhood social studies." In Seefeldt, C. (Ed.), *The early childhood curriculum: Current findings in theory and practice*, pp. 160–161. New York: Teachers College Press.

National Council of Teachers of Mathematics (NCTM). (1989). *Curriculum and evaluation standards for school mathematics*. Reston, VA: NCTM.

New York City Department of Education. (2003). *Prekindergarten performance standards*, pp. 15–16. New York: New York City Department of Education.

Schwartz, S. L. (1994). "Seasonal crafts: Discovering mathematical relationships and solving mathematical problems." *Teaching Children Mathematics* 1 (4): 214–219.

———. (2004). "Explorations in graphing with prekindergarten children." In Clarke, B., & Clark, D., et al., *International perspectives on learning and teaching mathematics*, pp. 83–97. Goteborg, Sweden: National Center for Mathematics Education.

Schwartz, S. L., & Robison, H. R. (1982). *Designing curriculum for early childhood*. Boston: Allyn and Bacon.

Seefeldt, C., & Galper, A. (2000). *Active experiences for active children: Social studies*. Upper Saddle River, NJ: Merrill.

Shilling, W. A., & Schwartz, S. L. (unpublished). "Child's world." Curriculum unit written for CUNY Literacy Project (City University of New York). Jamaica, NY: York College, CUNY. A curriculum implemented in priority schools in New York City.

Taylor, J. (1997). "Young children deal with data." *Teaching Children Mathematics* 4 (3): 146–149.

Webster's Collegiate Dictionary Tenth Edition. (1993). Springfield, MA: Merriam-Webster.

Whitin, D. (1997). "Collecting data with young children." *Young Children* 3 (5): 28–32.

Williams, L., & DeGaetano, Y. (1985). *ALERTA: A multicultural, bilingual approach to teaching young children*. Menlo Park, CA: Addison-Wesley.

CHAPTER 11

Meaningful Use of Mathematics in Classroom Routines

It was fifteen minutes into the free-choice center time, and children were involved in using materials and developing activities in all the interest centers in the classroom. Two children were studying the center chart which displayed pictures of each of the interest centers. Next to each center listed there was a fixed number of spaces to hold children's picture/name cards. The children were deeply engaged in counting the number of children's cards on the chart next to the block center. Of the six spaces available, five were filled. After they counted the picture/name cards, they turned and counted the number of children who were using materials in the block center. Discovering an inconsistency, five cards on the chart and only four children in the center, they began to figure out who was missing from the center. They did this by "reading" the picture/name cards and checking the center. Once they identified the missing classmate, they located her in another area and told her to come and change her card from the block area to the reading center where she now was. This left two spaces for these two children to enter the block center. They quickly placed their cards in the empty slots and proceeded to the center.

In this vignette, which repeated itself daily over the course of the early weeks of school in this kindergarten, the children were using their mathematical skills of counting and matching sets to negotiate their access to classroom resources. They were not conscious of "doing mathematics." Rather they were "using mathematics."

Events which make up a large part of the management of programs for young children include (1) recording attendance; (2) distributing materials (for example, serving foods during eating periods, and distributing classroom materials during curriculum activities); (3) providing fair and equitable access to the valued activities and resource materials in the classroom; (4) sharing responsibility for the classroom jobs that need to be done; and (5) maintaining the order of materials and equipment.

The difference between authentic use of mathematics and artificial practice rests in the children's view of the purpose for which the mathematics is used. If its use serves ongoing interests and activities, mathematics becomes an integral part of everyday living. When groups of children gather for different purposes, it can serve as a tool for improving the quality of life by enhancing children's autonomy in the management of the group activities, establishing the way responsibilities are shared, and determining how resources are allocated (Dacey & Eston 1999).

A major goal for young children centers on strengthening the self-concept through self-knowing, self-valuing and establishing a sense of membership in a group (Robison & Schwartz 1972). Social responsibility develops through the experience of being active participants in a social group in which the management system is sensible, reasonable, and equitable. Effective management procedures improve the quality of group life for children by fostering a sense of community and dignity for individuals. To achieve this end, the procedures need to

- inform children in formats they can understand,
- assure equity in access to classroom resources,
- facilitate children's active involvement in distribution of materials,
- arrange sharing of responsibility in an equitable way,
- protect individual rights for use of space and materials, and
- provide for differences in timing and pacing and development.

The following activities, in which mathematics serves an important function, have been designed by teachers of young children to provide them the opportunity to become increasingly responsible for managing their own social environment.

Recording and Using Attendance Data

Belonging to a group is an important experience for young children. The daily experience of figuring out which members of the group are missing helps build a sense of group membership. A variety of formats

Model of picture/name card for attendance chart:

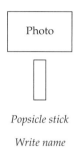

Popsicle stick

Store picture/name card in slot   *Write name*   *Move card to slot upon arrival*

Figure 11.1. Attendance Chart

allow children to complete this task with little or no help from adults. A simple format for an attendance chart (see Figure 11.1 for an example) helps children quickly learn how to enter the information without adult help, thereby placing them in a position to find their own ways to use it.

As children make daily entries, their interest begins with locating themselves on the list. Soon interest in the recorded information takes the form of comparing it with the information they get as they look around the classroom. Their growing sense of community with the group feeds the search for finding out who is absent and who is present. They may compare one-to-one, looking first at the children and then at the list or the reverse. In either case they are pairing items in the set of people with the list of group members as illustrated in the following conversation that was overheard in a prekindergarten class.

> Child 1: "Hey look. There's Pedro" (pointing to Pedro's picture/name card).
> Child 2: "Yeah. And he's over there with a puzzle" (pointing to Pedro in the classroom).
> Child 1: "I don't see Andrea" (looking around the room).
> Child 2: "Oh, yes, here's her card" (pointing to her picture/name card).
> Child 1: "Yeah. But she isn't here. See. She didn't move her card. And she isn't in the room" (pointing to the empty space where the card would be moved if the child had signified her attendance).

From the children's point of view, the process of identifying who is missing is their way of declaring that everyone is important. Further opportunities to use the name list occur when the group needs to figure out how to (1) organize milk and other foods for snack, (2) set up chairs for a special activity, or (3) adjust helper assignments to account for absent classmates.

The attendance chart provides easy access for obtaining and organizing the information for ongoing program activities, such as assignments for various daily chores which children enjoy performing, and long-term planning for trips and special class events.

Recording and Using Children's Choices for Interest Centers

The decision to design child-driven management procedures at center time grows out of a belief that the most effective way to support children's productive involvement in activities is to set up a system in which they can make choices. In the simplest and most direct procedure, the choice is signaled by obtaining a center tag in the form of a necklace as they enter a center. In the next level, children signal their choice by filling a designated space on a chart at the entrance to the center with their own picture/name card. In this case, the children are not wearing their choice, but rather have registered it at the site. A more distance format is the one illustrated in the vignette, where one chart centrally located represents all of the centers. In order to fulfill its purpose—allowing children to figure out if there is room to join the activity in the center—the procedure needs to be geared to children's developing ability to use mathematical thinking and read pictures and words.

The public information further equips the teacher to model ways to negotiate changes in location as children signal interest in changing centers. After one child expressed frustration that there was no room in the block center, the teacher suggested, "If you want to work in the block area, Sondra, why don't you find out if one of the children there wants to trade places with you?"

Using Mathematics in the Process of Distributing Snack Food and Utensils

The distribution of materials during the daily snacktime ritual provides a variety of opportunities for both spontaneous and adult stimulated counting and matching of sets. In order to effectively fulfill the role of table-server, it is essential to make sure that each member of the group receives the items in the snack service. Due to its daily occurrence and its high interest, the snack context provides a setting for posing computational problems at successively more advanced levels. The simplest level is that of adding one more, as when the adult says, "When you counted the children at your table, you counted four, but now Thomasina has joined the group. There were four and now there is one more, so how many napkins will you need?" The sequence of easier-to-harder problems is determined by both the size of the sets children are dealing with and the nature of the task.

The problem-setting in this natural context begins with simple addition, combining of sets and subtraction, or set-separation using sets under five, as illustrated above. Advancing to more complex problems of combining and separating sets that are larger than five or ten depends on finding out how children think through the mathematical problem. There is an ever-present need for the adult to inquire, "How did you figure that out?" in order to make decisions on the pattern of the next problem.

In one kindergarten class where the teacher had developed a ritual of posing mathematical problems for servers at snack time, the children's parents were reporting that the children were repeating the ritual at home, but reversing roles. They were challenging their parents to solve mathematical problems during the family set-up for eating and during eating periods. The parents were startled to find the children adding the explanatory information: "And do you know how I figured that out? First I . . . and then I. . . ."

In a recently reported project in Sweden, the teachers built children's understanding of and skill with fractions through daily distribution of fruit at snack time. Initially, the adults engaged each child in declaring how many pieces to make. The size of the pieces were not considered important at this beginning level. Over a period of time, the conversation moved to consideration of the size of the pieces and the use of the terms, "halves," "quarters," and "thirds" in natural contexts (Doverborg & Samuelsson 2000).

Concluding Remarks

In a management system devoted to fostering independence and responsibility, mathematics can serve as a tool to help children actively participate in developing and monitoring the procedures for living together.

References

Dacey, L. S., & Eston, R. (1999). *Growing mathematical ideas in kindergarten.* Sausalito, CA: Math Solutions.

Doverborg, E., & Samuelsson, I. (2000). "To develop young children's conception of numbers." *Early Childhood Development and Care* (162): 81–107.

"Ideas that work with young children." (Editors Column). (1987). "Child choice—Another way to individualize—Another form of preventive discipline." *Young Children* 43 (1): 48–54.

Robison, H. R., & Schwartz, S. L. (1972). *Learning at an early age*, vol. 2. Boston: Allyn and Bacon.

Schwartz, S. L. (1994). "Calendar reading: A tradition that begs remodeling." *Teaching Children Mathematics* 1 (2): 104–111.

CHAPTER 12

Putting It All Together

One Model

Shaping program activities to integrate the pursuit of valued curriculum goals is one of the most challenging and stimulating tasks that face educators. There is no rule that prescribes the beginning of an extended learning engagement for children. It can start unexpectedly when children are reading or listening to a story, manipulating and constructing with materials, completing a project, or following a group routine. Similarly, it can follow a predicted route begun by an adult-planned discussion or curriculum activity. The continuing message throughout this book is that, irrespective of the how new learning appears upon the scene, successful feeding of these emerging understanding and skills requires adult knowledge of how content builds in meaningful contexts for young children and the many faces of the steps along the way. The progressive stages discussed in previous chapters include

- Initial learning in the form of discovery that occurs in so many different kinds of situations that it would be difficult to make an exhaustive list. Sometimes the adult is present and can foster the awareness of mathematical relationships at the moment it begins. Other times, opportunities to validate and extend initial understandings occur intermittently over a period of time.
- Similarly, practice and application take form in activities initiated by children and ones shaped by the adult. *Self-initiated practice* occurs in diverse contexts, sometimes in an isolated repetitive set of actions, such as counting blocks over and over, and other times in a context in which counting serves a purpose, such as repeatedly

counting how many times one can bounce a ball. *Adult-shaped prac-tice* that has meaning to children ranges from playful imitative and interactive activities to structured games and projects involving re-peated patterns

- Application, the ability to use mathematical understandings and skills appropriately in context to meet the demands of daily living and to successfully pursue interests, constitutes our long-term goal. It requires the integration of mathematics with curriculum for early childhood.

Earlier chapters featured the ways in which mathematical fluency grows through adult fostering of discovery and practice in increasingly more complex activities. Supporting mathematical thinking and skills in integrated curriculum activities requires adult awareness of where the mathematics is embedded. This chapter presents a model of the inte-grated approach that furthers children's application of their mathemati-cal competencies as they increase their understanding of urban geography. It is presented as a unit with a sequence of activities that pro-vide opportunities for young children to begin to develop understanding of the big ideas that govern our understanding of the subject.

The Community as a Resource for the Geography Curriculum

No matter what kind of a community surrounds the school, explo-ration using concepts from geography serves as a naturally stimulating curriculum focus. Lucy Sprague Mitchell, author of *Young Geographers*, of-fers a vivid description of how she personally approached her study of human geography while taking a year off to work at the American Geo-graphic Society. She begins with learning from direct experience:

> For months I walked, street by street, across meadows, around the dump-ing grounds under the Queensboro Bridge, along the shore of the East River, a box of colored pencils hanging around my neck and maps in my hands. On photostats of real estate maps, I entered types of buildings in different colors—industrial buildings, stores, public utilities, public services, resi-dences—individual houses, two-family houses and apartment houses with stores under them. (Mitchell 1971, preface)

Her narrative continues with collecting information from population data, environmental reports, and historical demographics. Where she began suggests approaches to curriculum activities to develop geographic learnings in meaningful contexts with young children.

A Tale of Prekindergarten Children and Geography Study

A few years ago, one group of four-year-olds became enthusiastically involved in mapping experiences as a result of a series of focused observation walks. The experiences were spurred by conversations overheard by the adult when the children were constructing with blocks. Their adventure into geography and learning about land-surface use began with a walk up and down the school block to identify how many ways the land was being used. They found residential buildings, a church, storage buildings, garages, driveways, a street, and sidewalks. Subsequent walks which built on this introductory experience sought to answer such questions as "How far can we go without leaving the sidewalk?" and "How many streets do we have to cross to get to the pet store?" Very shortly after initiating these focused walks, the children's interest in geography began to show up in the block constructions. They used the blocks to build models for helping them work through their growing understanding of the geographic concepts associated with channels for movement—(1) streets or other vehicle pathways, (2) sidewalks, and (3) nodes or intersections of pathways. Not unexpectedly, intersections posed the greatest challenge to these children and held the greatest fascination.

A natural follow-up to investigating pathways and intersections is to find out how intersections are controlled. What rules are posted in the form of traffic lights and signs? If there are no posted rules, how is the traffic controlled to avoid collisions between people and inanimate objects? Observation walks in the neighborhood provide some answers to such questions as "What do vehicles do when coming out of a driveway, crossing walkways? Do they stop? Where? At the edge of sidewalk, or at the street edge?"

For these children, the adventure took an unexpected turn when they began to look at their block constructions from a mapper's view. They looked down on the roadways they constructed and engaged in discussions about location of buildings and distances from this vantage point. The teacher was able to arrange a trip to the viewing tower of a local church, which gave children an opportunity to look at the school and the surrounding local streets from an elevated position.

The engagement of these four-year-olds in the evolving geography unit revealed unanticipated capabilities for dealing with content not usually provided to children of this age. They used the mathematics of number, geometry, and measurement to support the ideas they were developing through the creation of models and maps to express their budding understanding.

Planning Curriculum Activities

The following list categorizes the organization of a geographical system and may be used to define the areas of focus for curriculum planning:

1. Land use by people: Land-surface use includes residential, commercial, recreational, and waste disposal. In addition, there are uncultivated areas and bodies of water which may or may not be actively used.

2. Movement from one place to another by people or objects (vehicles) and for transmitting information and ideas. Planned pathways designate the pattern of movement for people, objects, information, and ideas. The term *desire-lines* is used to identify the connection between the points where movements originate and terminate.

3. Channels, referring to the paths those movements take. For example, streets, bridges, elevators, stairs, hallways, and highways are all channels. So are telephone lines, telegraph lines, cables, the post office system, and air routes.

4. Intersections or nodes. Intersections, points where two or more channels meet or cross, may be grouped in terms of complexity or density and related economic factors. For example, an intersection in a city residential area might have one newsstand. In contrast, within an urban center there are likely to be multiple uses of the same site for such varied purposes as residential, commercial, professional, industrial, retail, entertainment, and transportation.

A further breakdown of these components is illustrated in a social studies article titled "Land-Use Patterns in the City" (Lampe and Schaefer 1974). The authors developed a seven-item category system which was intended primarily for looking at city land use:

1. Single-family residencies;
2. Multiple-family dwellings or apartments;
3. Commercial or business: retail, wholesale, and service;

4. Industrial, manufacturing, and railroads;

5. Public: schools, government functions, parks, and churches;

6. Streets; and

7. Vacant and unused lands (Lampe & Schaefer 1974).

Prototype of a Geography Unit

Preparing: Studying the Neighborhood. Each community is unique. A careful review of the resources in the local neighborhood is needed to begin the process.

Launching the Unit. Tables 12.1 and 12.2 offer a guide to launch and develop a neighborhood study unit that can be tailored to accommodate the range of early childhood, prekindergarten through grade 2. Content can be adapted to build on children's prior experiences in terms of knowledge and skills.

Critical components of the recommended activities include:

- connecting to children's interests;
- coordinating the learning processes with children's prior knowledge and skill development;
- embedding literacy throughout to support the growth in understanding from intuitive to conscious knowing: discussion, keeping records, searching for more information in the literature; and
- helping children validate and extend through review and further independent and guided experiences.

Extending the Unit. Identify one more topic based on observations of children's interests and level of expertise in developing geographic understandings about structures and movement channels. You may find that their interests lead to

- further experiences in mapping beyond the local street area: making models of different neighborhoods or a favorite park, using mapping skills to plan trips or report on a travel experience;
- the study of scientific aspects of the environment: examining balance in land use in terms of food sources, conservation issues, or patterns of erosion related to land use; and
- the history of changes in structures related to community needs.

Table 12.1
Urban Geography: Structures and Land Use

Big Ideas
People build structures for different purposes
Structures vary in architectural details; size, shape, windows, doors, rooftops

Resources
Local structures for dwellings, homes, businesses, recreation, education
Books and magazines

Context
Children's expressed interest in examining and representing structures using such materials as blocks, manipulatives, arts and crafts, pictures and books. May be provoked by listening to a story on looking at picture books, or by a curriculum unit/theme or project.

Activity Possibilities and Instructional Strategies	Sample Content Acquisition and Skill Development
Discussion: Initiate group discussion to pursue children's interests, expressed in activities such as constructing and drawing pictures of structures. Elicit perceptions about size, shape, and purposes of buildings they list. With children, make a list of what they have seen on their way to school or in their own neighborhoods. Invite children to help enter information on the list, drawing pictures or making other kinds of entries. If needed, use a book or pictures of structures to stimulate further conversation about structures and their uses.	*Literacy*: Oral language, vocabulary, and expressing ideas. *Social studies*: Increase of knowledge about urban structures and their purposes; recording data. *Mathematics*: Using number, space, and locational geometry and comparative size measurement to describe observations
Walking trips: Propose a walking trip to look at building structures in the local school area, on the school street or around school block. The first task is to observe and compare structures in terms of size: number of windows, doors, shape of roof, and building materials, and also relate the structure to how it is used.	
Recording data: Provide clipboards and writing tools for children to record observations. NOTE: For those children who have never recorded observations, elicit possibilities and engage them in illustrating their ideas about different ways to record and remember observations about attributes of buildings.	

Table 12.1 (continued)

Activity Possibilities and Instructional Strategies

Sample Content Acquisition and Skill Development

Discussion during trip: Validate children's observations, to stimulate sharing and extend observations. Include adult observations in authentic manner, without distracting children's discoveries.

Recording data, using graphics, number and text; expanding and using descriptive vocabulary; learning through sharing observations; improving oral communication skills.

Discussion and follow-up activities after trip: Elicit from children what they observed and how they recorded it.
With children, create a group chart of their observations.
Chart may take the form of unsorted listing of pictures and words or web with pictures and words.
With children, reread recorded information. Encourage summarizing information that has been recorded. If information is difficult to retrieve, pose the option of finding a more efficient way to represent the data. Help children organize information for a more efficient data record (second chart).
Review information on the group chart for additions and omissions.
Engage children in thinking about "what else?"

General: Recording and organizing recorded data; reading recorded data.
Literacy: Communicating information in oral and written form.
Vocabulary building: Using descriptive language and geographic terms.
Social studies: Increasing knowledge about habitats and purposes of community structures.
General: Developing research skills.

For individual follow-up: (in interest centers for nonunit related trip): Provide block construction materials, craft materials, and books for children to pursue interest in structures. Observe and record children's use of trip observations to identify ways to *feed*, *seed* and *lead*. *Feed* by validating and extending through conversation during and at completion of activity. *Seed* by providing additional materials that children can choose to extend their activity related to structures. *Lead* by adding new content through discussion, read-alouds, and sharing children's work.
For unit/theme/project related activity: engage in follow-up activities related to purpose of trip.

Geography: Constructing models of observations for increased understanding.
Mathematics: Using number, geometry, and measurement relationships in construction of models.
Literacy: Expressing ideas and exchanging views; using language labels and descriptive terms in geography and mathematics.
In addition to the above: Using literature resources to extend knowledge.

Table 12.1 (continued)

Activity Possibilities and Instructional Strategies	Sample Content Acquisition and Skill Development
Plan next steps with children—for example, unit focused on people habitats, plan to produce models of different kinds of habitats, e.g., single and multiple dwellings; one floor, multiple floors, and create text to explain the models. With children, plan closing activity—presentation to other groups, a book, or a montage.	
Ending the curriculum segment: Review experiences and consider possibilities for collecting more information. For those involved in independent follow-up, take photos of their products for group discussion and create a library book for future use. *Extending the experiences*: Plan further trips and other ways collect information, answer questions, and report findings to questions that children listed.	*Literacy*: Using literature resources; writing and illustrating reports to share. *Geography*: Clarifying understandings. *Science*: Examining the relationship between human use of land and effects on community resources.

Irrespective of the curriculum focus, think in terms of the related curriculum learnings that are embedded in the process. Use Table 12.3 to plan the next set of experiences.

Concluding Remarks

Mathematics is an academic subject in its own right. However, for young children, mathematical understanding and skills develop most effectively when learned and used in contexts that have meaning and importance to them. Effective support for mathematics learning requires (1) knowledge of the big ideas that are integral to mathematics content sequences, (2) familiarity with the ways in which children demonstrate their mathematics capabilities, from discovery of patterns and relationships to planful use of mathematics as a tool to accomplish their goals, (3) the

Table 12.2
Urban Geography: Movement Pathways

Big Ideas
Streets and sidewalks are major pathways for movement of humans, animals, and vehicles.
Forms, speed and direction of movement vary.
Street and sidewalk pathways intersect.
Collisions may occur at intersections.
Signals to monitor movement at intersections reduce the likelihood of collisions.
Other pathways exist for communication purposes: telephone and electric lines; mailboxes; fire call boxes and phone booths; television antennas.

Resources
Local streets, sidewalks, and driveways
Communication channels and sites
Books and community personnel

Context
Follows experiences related to structures and land use in the local community.

Activity Possibilities and Instructional Strategies	Sample Content Acquisition and Skill Development
Group discussion (prior to trip): Recall prior trip(s) to view structures. Raise question about other forms of land use besides structures—e.g., open spaces, movement pathways.	*Literacy*: vocabulary development, geographic terms, and descriptive language.
Refer to children's block constructions of roadways, train tracks, and general manipulation of miniature vehicles.	*Social Studies*: increased understanding of land use in urban settings; awareness of need for monitoring movement along different pathways for safety purposes; recording, summarizing and analyzing data.
Propose a walking trip to look at movement along pathways.	
Locale walking trips: Provide children with clipboards and writing tools to record their observations.	*Mathematics*: Use of number, location, direction, and intersections in geometry; linear measurement to represent data.
During trip: Elicit from children what they are seeing and how they are recording their observations. Create a group chart of information.	

Table 12.2 (continued)

Activity Possibilities and Instructional Strategies	Sample Content Acquisition and Skill Development
After trip: Discuss what children observed and share their (data) recordings. *Interest center activity*: Extend conversation during children's use of blocks and other construction materials. Encourage children to invent different ways to control movement at intersections. Photograph children's products for review and discussion. *Project related activities*: With children, plan follow-up activities related to project: e.g., making models of observed pathways, using construction materials; drawing pictures to illustrate events on pathways, dramatizing movement on pathways, preparing a message to mail, collecting and illustrating geography words. Photograph products for making group book or display. *Feed* by engaging in conversation with children during process. *Seed* by providing necessary resources for children to extend the activity. *Lead* by sharing new content and reviewing content already accumulated on charts and through experience.	*Geography*: Awareness of events at intersections and problem solving. *Mathematics*: Use of number, location, direction, and intersections in geometry; linear measurement to make models of observed intersections. *Mathematics*: Transforming two-dimensional drawings into three-dimensional representations, or the reverse. *Literacy*: Oral language fluency; creating written labels for models, drawings. *Reading*: source material.
Follow-up trips: Discover some communication pathways: e.g., telephone and electrical lines, mail boxes, phone booths, fire call boxes. Select focus based on children's interests. Elicit prior knowledge about ways people communicate. Pursue information in one area at a time after initial discovery of the different communication channels observed in the local environment. E.g., study the postal system, identifying the sequence of movement from initial mailing of letter to it destination.	*Literacy*: Writing, collecting information; reading source material; oral fluency. *Geography*: increased knowledge about communication systems. *Mathematics*: Consideration of measurement of time in communication.

Table 12.3
Curriculum Activity Planner

Big Ideas
-
-

Resources
-
-

Context
-
-

Activity Possibilities and Instructional Strategies	Sample Content Acquisition and Skill Development

kinds of activities that will further their active use of number, geometry, measurement, data collection, and (4) understanding of the instructional strategies that contribute to children's learning of mathematics in contexts that are meaningful to them.

Recommended Reading

Bacon, P. (Ed.). (1970). *Focus on geography: Key concepts and teaching strategies.* 40th Yearbook. Washington, DC: National Council for the Social Studies. Premise of the book is that "geography and human behavior have become vital partners" if humans are to survive on earth. In response to and as part of this awareness, geography has undergone a dynamic change, to which educators of the young can direct attention. A serious attempt is made to translate complex ideas in geography into simpler terms, making geography more intelligible to the nongeographer. Features historical and current aspects of interdependence of economic, social, cultural, and geographic forces of an area. This book has a great deal to offer to a student of sociology, anthropology, economics, geography, or environmental science, or teacher education.

Elementary Science Study (ESS Project). (1971). *Teacher's guide for mapping*. Newton, MA: Education Development Center, Inc. This out-of-print teacher's guide is worth searching for. It provides comprehensive information and instructions for all the steps in the process of developing children's understanding of the purposes and functions of maps as well as directions for producing three-dimensional map models and converting them to graphic representations. It also includes mapping games.

Sobel, D. (1998). *Mapmaking with children: Sense-of-place education for the elementary years*. Portsmouth, NH: Heinemann. The descriptions of mapping activities are specified in separate chapters for the different age groups, beginning with five- and six-year-olds. The author focuses on "curriculum that mirrors development." The final segment of the book looks at ways for "exploring hidden landscapes" through literature and the exploration of "special places." This book offers a rich set of ideas for mapmaking with children in meaningful contexts.

References

Jarolimek, J., & Walsh, H. (Eds). (1974). *Reading for social studies in elementary education*. 3rd ed. New York: Macmillan.

Lampe, F., & Schaefer, O. (1974). "Land-use patterns in the city." In Jarolimek, J., & Walsh, H. (Eds.), *Readings for social studies in elementary education*, pp. 409–411. New York: Macmillan.

Mitchell, L. (1953). *Two lives*. New York: Simon and Schuster. As quoted in preface of reprint of *Young geographers* (1971). New York: Bank Street College of Education.

Index

The letter *t* following a page number denotes a table.

About the Author

SYDNEY L. SCHWARTZ is Professor Emerita, Elementary and Early Childhood Education, Queens College, City University of New York. She publishes extensively in her field of mathematics education.